THE RECKONING

THE RECKONING

TARA PROFFITT
WITH SUNDAY TIMES BESTSELLING AUTHOR
ANN CUSACK

MIRROR BOOKS

MIRROR BOOKS

All of the events in this story are true, but some names and details have been changed to protect the identities of individuals.

1

Published in Great Britain and Ireland in 2026 by Mirror Books, a Reach PLC business.

Photographic Acknowledgements: Alamy

www.mirrorbooks.co.uk
@TheMirrorBooks

Print ISBN 9781917439817
eBook ISBN 9781917439824

Editing and Production: Christine Costello
Cover Design: Adam Ward

Printed and bound in Great Britain by
CPI Group (UK) Ltd, Croydon, CR0 4YY

FSC www.fsc.org MIX Paper | Supporting responsible forestry FSC® C013604

I dedicate this book to my parents Alison Connolly and Nicholas Heys and to every soul struggling with trauma, abuse and breaking the chain.

To the life lesson that made me the mother and very soul I am today. To the souls lost without a voice carrying guilt, shame or suffering that is not yours to carry.

Let me be your voice until you feel strong enough to use yours. I hope this book brings you clarity, love and peace. We are not defined by pain – it made us who we are.

Pain is power!

Prologue

MAY 2015, SWINDON

THE IDEA had only just popped into my head. Yet at the same time, it had always been there, lying dormant like a winter seed. And now, as the plan unfurled and bloomed in my mind, I felt close, so close, to justice.

"He's in the pub," Uncle Tommy told me. "Just two pints. A creature of habit, you know what he's like."

Yes, I knew my grandfather's routine better than anyone. He'd be home soon after 7pm and I would be there waiting. Gripping my phone tightly in my trouser pocket, I ran through the plan, over and over.

Oddly, I was not at all afraid of confronting him. My fear of my grandfather was linked to a shame which had vanished the day my mother was murdered and was replaced by a cold, hard anger.

Now, it was my job to get to the truth for her. Rounding the corner into my grandfather's street, I spotted the house with its four dark windows: four black eyes framed by a glowering face. I could almost taste the menace, the foreboding, even before I reached the gate. The back door would be on the latch; again, I knew his routine well. Yet as I made my way down the alleyway, my blood froze in my veins.

The door was a portal into past misery. I was suddenly six years old again; a slight, frightened little girl, stepping into a monster's lair. I was gripped by a crazy notion that the house might reach out with spindly arms, gather me up and swallow me whole. This place clamped its jaws around you and didn't let you leave. The house, it seemed, terrified me far more than the abuser himself.

"Do it for Mum, Tara," I reminded myself. "Do it for Mum."

On jelly legs, I somehow propelled myself through the kitchen, noting the gleaming draining board, the tea-towel neatly folded, the washing machine humming quietly. To the outside world, this was a normal home; clean, tidy, well-kept. Yet there was a darkness, a thick, choking malevolence, which clung to my clothes and made it hard for me to breathe.

"Do it for Mum," I whispered.

Before arriving, I had told myself I would check each room in the house; partly to make sure it was empty but more so as a show of defiance, if only to myself.

I am not afraid to be here.

Even so, as I crept along the patterned carpet of the hallway, past the pictures of Elvis and the old-fashioned ornaments, my resolve shivered. This house was a witness, yes, but it was more than that. There was a complicity in the way Elvis stared back at me and in the groan of the old floorboards.

She's here. She's back again.

Upstairs, the front bedroom was cold and almost empty. Yet in a flash I saw myself and Grampy. Me, six years old and terrified, but believing this was what happened in families. That this was just how it was. I shook my head hard to dislodge the memory and closed the door.

"You can do it. You can do it."

This time, it was Mum's voice, urging me on from beyond the grave. Later, I had dozens of sandwiches to make, and sausage rolls to cook, ready for her wake. But this was the real closure, the real reckoning, right here. Next, the bathroom. Familiar blue walls, creamy white sink, toilet and bath.

Again, I'd thought it was perfectly normal when Grampy came in to wash me, locking the door behind him. I remembered how the birdsong had lifted me up gently and out through the open window, how I had shut my eyes as I flew away with the birds to safety.

Twenty years later, I was still sleeping with the bedroom window open so I could listen to the comforting sound of the birds. I took a moment to steady myself, leaning on the sink whilst I pulled together the thin threads of courage I had left.

"You can do it," Mum whispered again, and I nodded weakly.

"I know," I replied. "I know. And I won't let you down."

Downstairs, I sank onto the tatty cream sofa, clutching a

cushion to me like a shield. The house was energy-sapping, vampire-like. I felt almost drugged. Just being here made me feel heavy and dragged down. Yet I was strangely wired too. My disquiet bled into the sofa; an electric current of panic passing through each piece of furniture.

My eyes travelled over more Elvis pictures adorning every wall. This place was like a cult. Nobody left unscathed. And then, in the corner, I spotted it. A small, faded photo of Mum, taken when she was in high school. She was so pretty, so innocent. Even by then, she'd been ripped to shreds inside. Yet from her vulnerability, as always, I drew my strength.

"I can do it," I told her firmly.

And once again, my resolve was set. I set my phone on record and placed it on a cushion to my left. I had been waiting around 20 minutes when I heard the door open. Strangely, as my grandfather came into the living room, he didn't seem too surprised to see me. He looked older, after all these years. He'd lost his hair too. But behind the glasses were the same ice-cold eyes which had haunted my nightmares for so long. We stared at one another, the silence rising to a crescendo, until he cracked first, as I had hoped he would.

"I know, I know, I didn't go to the funeral," he said, swatting my complaints away before I could make them. I steeled myself.

"Do you really think that's why I'm here, Grampy, because

you missed Mum's funeral?" I asked. "I'm here because you wrecked her life. You sexually abused her, didn't you, right from being a small child?"

The truth shot out like a cannonball across the room. I was swamped by a whirlpool of serrated memories, an angry mess of pain and shame. Each word was like a blade dragging across my skin.

"Yes," he said, his head dropping as his guilt crackled around him. "I did."

Momentarily, I was wrong-footed. I hadn't expected him to fold like this. It was almost as though he'd been waiting to confess. Anger surged through me, but I reminded myself to stay calm. I didn't want a defence barrister accusing me of forcing a confession. I drew in a sharp breath.

"You abused me too, didn't you?" I continued.

"I did," he confirmed. "I'm sorry."

Somehow, that annoyed me more than anything. Sorry? What use was that? Sorry that Mum's life was torn apart by her own father's abuse and that she had been murdered? Sorry that I had hauled a sack of shame and guilt around since I was six years old? Sorry that when I woke screaming with night terrors, I saw the face of my own grandfather, and not my partner, lying on the pillow next to me? Sorry that his filthy secret had gnawed away at us both, resonating through our existence like a death knell?

"Sorry?" I repeated, my voice hard as granite. "What help is that to me?"

"I know it's wrong," he said glibly, the words tripping off his tongue as though he was reading from a book.

Again, I was filled with a poker-hot fury; the rage like an animal fighting to get out of my chest. He knew it was wrong, he said he was sorry, and yet he had continued, days, months, years of sickening, stomach-churning abuse. His own daughter. His own granddaughter. Shaking with revulsion, I focussed on Mum's photo, smiling back at me, and I somehow swallowed down my anger again.

"Mum was the best thing in my life, and you took her from me," I told him. "I blame you for it all. She would not have been murdered if you hadn't abused her. She would have been a different person altogether."

He made no move to disagree, and again, that enraged me more than if he'd tried to defend himself.

"I'm recording all of this," I snapped, shocking myself and him by waving my phone in the air. "You're being filmed. I'm going to the police."

I strode past him, my heart ablaze with fury and pride. My apprehension was long gone. I had faced him, I had confronted him, and I had snared him.

"You were always different, Tara," sighed my grandfather, as I reached the door.

"Yes," I replied. "And here is the difference with me. I will see justice done."

1

SUMMER 1997, 11PM

I WOKE with a jolt so brutal it was like a physical punch. Downstairs, someone was yelling and hammering on the front door. Mum started to wail, Dad's panicked voice quickly drowning out hers. And then a big smash; a shower of shattering glass and angry threats.

"You owe us! Last chance to pay up!"

I was on the top bunk with my little sister, Jasmine. My two younger siblings were on the bunk below. At 10, I was the eldest and though sick with fear, I knew I had to take charge.

"Here," I whispered, throwing the bedsheet up over our heads. "Climb inside my tent. Let's go camping!"

I managed to hook the sheet onto the wooden corners of the bunkbeds to give us some height. We helped the younger ones up the ladder and the four of us huddled together in our makeshift tent. It was too risky to make any noise. Instead, I sent a silent beam of reassurance from my eyes to theirs, a lighthouse in the darkness of our young lives.

"Have the bad men gone, Tar?" Jasmine whispered, her small hand gripping mine.

"They're leaving soon," I promised. "You're safe in our tent."

I waited until she was curled up asleep with the other two before creeping down the ladder. It was quiet downstairs now, but my heart was a clenched fist. I had to check on my mum, Alison, to make sure she wasn't hurt – or worse. From the living room, I heard a low whimper and found her cowering on the mattress where she and my dad, Nick, slept. He was long gone, running at the first sight of trouble and leaving Mum to face it alone. There was a cold draught from the broken window, and I had to tiptoe carefully over shards of glass in my bare feet. Mum held her arms up towards me like a baby waiting to be cradled.

"It's okay," I soothed, as though she was one of the little ones. "It's over now."

We huddled on the mattress together and she sobbed. I held her hand and the love flowed like liquid gold between us; through my fingers and into hers. I was so relieved she was unharmed, but at the same time the weight of responsibility was crushing. At 10 years old, I was the mother-figure in this house of chaos; this terrifying existence where we were not safe even in our own beds at night. Both of my parents were addicts and, though I would not fully understand the reasons for many years, the consequences were laid bare for me every day. There was nothing to cushion me when I fell, no arms to catch me and fold around me when disaster struck – and it always did. But this was not about me.

"I don't know what I'd do without you, Tar," Mum said quietly as I began sweeping the glass into a pile at the side of the sofa. "I really don't."

Ever since I could remember, she had been vulnerable and fragile. As a small child I'd sensed, instinctively, that she needed to be looked after. And as the eldest one left at home, the role seemed to fit me perfectly, whether I liked it or not. Mum's life bumped along in an uneven cycle, five or six catatonic days in bed, followed by three or four days up and about, before she retreated under her duvet again. I didn't understand what trauma or mental illness was; where it had come from or if it might one day go away again. As a toddler, I just thought Mum was very tired and I longed for her to wake up and play. Yet by the time I started school, I was beginning to understand it was more than that. There was a sadness clinging to her skin, an air of desolation, of defeat. Even in her own home, with her family around her, she looked completely lost. In the night, she'd cry out in agony, and though I was half-asleep, I could never ignore her. Hurrying down the bunkbed ladder, I'd take a cold flannel downstairs to the living room, knowing she'd be soaked through with sweat. Still half-asleep, she mumbled and groaned as I wiped her face and held her hand.

"I'm here, Mum," I told her.

Even when I was very small, she was never: 'Mummy.' The

name implied a level of care and nurturing which was alien to my mother. She loved us all dearly; I was in no doubt about that. But she could never show it. She didn't know how; she looked only inwards, a prisoner of her own sorrow, completely incapable of reaching out, even to her own child. Instead, our roles were reversed, and she relied on me to mother her. I just accepted that was how life was. Somehow, I struggled along on my own, looking after myself and the little ones as they each came along.

Every time Mum fell pregnant, I'd feel a rush of excitement followed by a dull thump, like a stone landing in my stomach. As much as I loved babies, I knew that another life translated into more work, more responsibility and more worry for me. Mum didn't concern herself with the future, she took each day as it came and seemed to like being pregnant because of the unusual attention from Dad. He fussed over her, indulging her cravings, nipping to the shop late at night for a bag of crushed ice or a packet of fruit pastilles.

Mostly my siblings were born at home, not out of choice or emergency, but simply because of the lack of planning or scheduling of any kind. There was no such thing as 'tomorrow' in our house. We lived for today; not in a carefree, easy-going way but because today was all we could cope with. Today was as far ahead as my parents could see. Life was a chaotic collection of disjointed chunks; there was no continuity, no fluidity, no joined up thinking at all. My mother would happily go off to hospital to give birth if someone sorted it out for her. Otherwise she gave birth at home because that was where she happened to be at the time. After each new baby arrived, a swarm of social workers descended like summer midges on our house, murmuring the same, well-worn phrases as last time:

With the mother's drug addiction to consider…

And there have been concerns from school…

Father also involved in drug dealing…

I felt like a case study, a specimen, of only mild interest to these professionals, who perched uneasily on our sofa and peered at us, before scurrying off and leaving behind the same mess as before. Sometimes, as they put on their coats, I felt like screaming at the top of my voice:

"We need help! I'm too young for all of this! We can't live on cereal for every meal!"

But I was well versed in family loyalty and knew better than to open my mouth to a stranger. Besides, Dad could not wait to usher the social workers and health visitors out of the house. He desperately needed support but could not or would not accept it. He didn't seem able to look after his children, yet he didn't want social services to help him either. He contributed to family life as much as he felt was necessary and by default, everything else was left to me.

In the mornings, I was up first, stepping carefully around the mattress where my parents were flat out as though I was picking my way through landmines. When Mum was asleep, whether it was for eight hours or eight days, she expected to be left in peace. Though she was never at peace, even when she was asleep, crying out in anguish in her nightmares, her hair and nightie soaked with sweat.

Occasionally, if Dad wasn't there and we had no clean clothes or I couldn't find a hairbrush, I might risk disturbing her before we left for school. But it was like poking a grizzly bear. She was so disorientated and angry that I instantly regretted asking her for help. Like Mum's, Dad's body clock was also ruled by drugs, but set in a different pattern. He was often up most of the night, and so he'd keep himself occupied by laying out our clothes and leaving a loaf out in the kitchen. Sometimes he got up even before me or perhaps hadn't been to bed at all. He might warm a piece of bread on the gas fire for us, and that was the closest we got to toast.

We had an electric grill but quite often, we had no electricity. No sooner was one utility reconnected than another red bill dropped through the letterbox and something else was cut off. And finding a small space to butter our warm bread required sweeping aside the drugs paraphernalia and empty lager cans which littered every downstairs surface. On special days, we had Lucky Charms cereal. It was very rare to find a day when we had both cereal and fresh milk. These were simple pleasures, but I treasured them all the more because of that and Lucky Charms made me feel very lucky indeed.

When I went into the juniors, I was trusted to take myself and the younger ones to school. But in my early years, Dad was usually ready to walk with us on the 10-minute journey from our home in Swindon. I hated leaving Mum behind, cocooned inside a thin duvet on that grubby mattress, with the little ones tottering uncertainly nearby. We had no carpets, only forgotten scraps of wallpaper, and the garden was crammed with black bin bags, waiting for someone else to take them away. That was my parents' approach to everything; someone else would take responsibility. Whatever the problem, and there always was one, it wasn't theirs. And so, almost by osmosis, the problems became mine.

I was responsible for the whole house. And each morning, as I closed the door behind me, my stomach twisted with worry. The house was not safe for the children. Mum could not cope without me. How would they manage on their own? By the time we reached the school gates, my anxiety was setting thick like concrete around me.

'Please don't leave me here,' I pleaded silently. 'I need to be at home looking after Mum and the babies. I need to keep them safe.'

But Dad was too busy with his own problems to worry about mine.

"I didn't ask for this," he complained as he hurried us along. "I didn't want all these kids. I can't be doing with you all."

His words heaped more blame and self-reproach onto my shoulders. My worries stacked up into a staircase of anxiety, ready to tumble down on top of me at any moment. Was all this really my fault, simply for being born? Was it just a case of numbers? I didn't see what I could do about that. I walked through the playground racked with guilt, almost bent double with shame. And as all the other children received goodbye hugs from their mothers, I stared at my scuffed shoes and blinked back tears. I knew better than this, better than to feel sorry for myself. Everyone was relying on me, I reminded myself. I needed to be stronger. Yet I felt so out of place lining up in the yard, when I should have been at home tidying away the breakfast pots and keeping an eye on my sisters.

In the classroom, I was as awkward and as out of place as a harassed young mother, perched on a small school chair whilst I fretted incessantly. I enjoyed my schoolwork. But what use were cursive writing and phonics lessons to me, when what I really needed were instructions on how to set off a hot wash and how long to boil pasta for? I enjoyed writing but I felt it had no place in my life, and I had nothing in common with these other kids. I felt isolated and far removed from their worlds, whilst at once being desperate to join in and be accepted. I coveted their freedom and their naivety, so desperately that, conversely, I pushed it away.

At playtimes, I locked myself away in the toilet block, telling myself I didn't want to mix with anyone. But in truth it was mostly self-preservation, and I was avoiding the awful truth that nobody wanted to play with me and their parents had marked me out as a child to avoid all costs.

The druggies' daughter… she's not a suitable friend for you… stay away…

Once, I'd plucked up courage to knock on a neighbour's door where a girl my age lived. When her mother answered she looked visibly offended and said, "My daughter would never hang around with your sort!" before slamming the door in my face.

It was one thing to label myself an outcast but another thing for others to do so, and I was mortified. But again, I could not allow myself to get upset and instead I forced a smile as I made my way back down the street, trying to pretend it had never happened.

From a young age, I developed the skill of rewriting reality, of stepping into a new, easier character, and leaving my old self behind. Back in class after playtime, I sat quietly, anxious not to draw attention to myself and determined to play a well-practised and low-key role of slotting in alongside the other children and keeping my secrets to myself. I felt like a puppet, stuck with no say over what happened to me.

"How are you today, Tara?" asked my teacher, Miss Bond, with a smile. "What did you have for breakfast?"

"Nothing," I wanted to say. "There was no food in the house, and my mother was asleep on the mattress when I left and I'm so worried about her it gives me a tummy ache. We have drug dealers banging on our doors wanting money, but I think my dad has spent it all. When they come back, they might kill us all. That's what Mum told me."

Instead, I ignored the clamour of voices in my head and replied, "Lucky Charms, Miss."

I had been raised to keep my mouth shut and I knew not to speak out and not to give way to the panic which simmered under my skin. My parents had drilled this into me; their instructions tattooed onto the inner lining of my mind. When the police came, when the dealers came, when the social workers came, we stayed quiet. When everyone had left, we could scream as loudly as we liked, and my parents often did.

"Perhaps," Miss Bond suggested. "You might like to come to my office at the next breaktime? I think I have an apple and a chocolate bar waiting for you."

Her eyes twinkled and I felt myself smile. I'd thought I was fooling everyone, acting out the part of a normal child. But perhaps Miss Bond wasn't taken in after all. In the lunch queue later, I was grateful for the snacks, because a dinner lady discreetly pulled me aside to say my parents had once again failed to sign my form for free school meals.

"I'm sorry, Tara, we can't give you any lunch," she said. "This is the third time it's happened. You need to remind your mother to return the form."

I stared at her blankly. My mother was asleep all the time. She wasn't a form-filling kind of mother. I wasn't even sure we had a pen in the house. But how to explain that? And how was this my responsibility, on top of everything else? I nodded obediently and trailed away down the corridor, to the sanctuary of the toilet block. I locked myself in a cubicle, trying and failing to regulate the anxiety which hovered over me like a shimmer of unbearable heat on a hot day. I worried constantly.

In class that afternoon, I watched the clock intently. I had learned before any of my classmates to tell the time, so that I knew when I could go home. 2pm, had anyone fed the little ones? 2.30pm, was Mum asleep? Were the little ones playing outside, near a road? Were they climbing on chairs or playing with matches? 2.45pm, had the police been again? Had Mum been arrested? Was she safe? Was my family about to implode? Was I going into care? When the final bell of the day rang out, I was flooded with relief, overcome with a desire to run home as fast as I could. But first, I had to wait for an adult. The irony of relying on the grown-ups in my life wasn't lost on me, even at that age. Sometimes, Dad was waiting in the playground to collect me, but sometimes he wasn't. I was used to being the last child remaining, and I approached the problem with quiet defiance rather than self-pity.

"I know my way home, I can walk myself, and take my sister," I insisted to Miss Bond. "I'm allowed out on my own, I promise."

But she wouldn't hear of it, and, after a few phone calls, Dad made an appearance, his lop-sided smile and hazy focus confirming he'd had his daily dose of cannabis. I could smell him before I saw him, the pungent scent of weed drifting across the school yard. Cringing, I knew I smelled the same too because some of the other kids took great delight in pointing that out. Yet there was nothing I could do; our home reeked of the stuff. It seeped from our pores like sweat. Drugs were a necessary evil in our home, as integral as food and certainly more important.

My parents could both go without food all day, but drugs were non-negotiable. I was conflicted; as much as I understood drugs were wrong, they were the only way of moderating Dad's tempers and Mum's anxieties. And mornings were the perfect example. Without his morning bong, Dad was tetchy and irritable, angry that my mother was sleeping, angry that he had too many children, angry that he was left to do the school run on his own. Mum, if woken, would be bewildered, weeping and swearing. Some mornings the mood was so brittle and aggressive that we had to leave. I'd guide the littles outside in their nighties to wait on the street corner for 10 or 15 minutes until our parents calmed down. And certainly by the afternoon, when they were stoned and mellow, there was at least a temporary harmony within the house. It was a patchy, fickle, sort of routine, consistent only in its inconsistency, but it was all we had.

Today, as I arrived home from school, Mum had moved upstairs to sleep in one of the bedrooms and the mattress was upended and leaning against the living room wall. Dad seemed reasonably content. He put on a Pink Floyd album whilst he made a shopping list on the back of a Rizla packet.

We never had food in the cupboards. On a good day, he'd go to the shops, buying only for that day and no further. He was a decent cook too; he could rustle up a spaghetti bolognese, noodles, sausage and chips. I loved the smell of dinner cooking; it was a phony confirmation of the normality I craved.

"Tara, wash these dishes, we've nothing clean," he shouted.

As I washed up, my arms deep in soap suds, I allowed my mind to wander. I ignored the drugs and the balled-up cash on the kitchen worktop, I avoided Dad's slightly glazed expression, I blocked out the sound of Mum softly weeping upstairs, and I pretended, for a moment, that we were just an ordinary family. Again, I was auditioning for a role, acting out a part, which one day I hoped might become my reality.

"Dinner's ready!" Dad yelled, and we all scrambled to the table.

I lifted the two smallest into highchairs, and the others found a place on the sofa. Even the little ones understood that the food would be gone in minutes, and there would be nothing else. Dad had not shopped beyond this one meal. He would not, or could not, see past the now. Little surprise that there were no holidays when we couldn't even plan ahead for a weekly shop. And it was not a lack of money; the bundles of tenners on the sideboard were testament to that. It was, instead, a total absence of care. We didn't make arrangements or organise events or plan treats, because nobody could be bothered to do so. The dirty dishes after our meal were piled up in the sink to be washed only when they were needed again. And soon, it was time for Dad and me to get the little ones into bed.

"Come on," I chivvied, taking Jasmine's hand in mine. "I'll run a bath and then I'll read you a story."

Dad followed me upstairs, collecting the dirty clothes ready for the wash. I squirted shower gel into the bath, fluffed up some bubbles with my hands, and plonked the two youngest into the water. Dad appeared at my shoulder, and I smiled at him.

"All clean," I announced.

But far from him welcoming my help, I felt the resentment, prickling like static, between us. He always seemed angry with me, always ready to lash out. He brought the night-clothes into the bathroom and hurried the little ones into the bedroom.

"No, Dad," I told him. "They need to clean their teeth first."

"I'm the father, you're the child," he said, clipping me round the back of the head. "Children should be seen and not heard. You'd do well to remember that."

"Children should be seen and not hurt," I retorted, knowing and not caring that I would get another slap for my insolence.

Despite my inner anxiety, I was a feisty kid, always ready to stand up for Mum and my siblings. Dad nicknamed me: 'Miss Angelica' after the bossy character in the *Rugrats*. And he was right. I had my priorities in order. I was forever telling him not to take drugs, not to leave them around the house, not to let strangers through our door.

"None of your business," he snapped. "Do as you're told."

But I couldn't help speaking up. I was the physical aspect of his conscience, sitting on his shoulder, pecking at his ear and pointing out what he was doing wrong. I knew I was wasting my breath, but I did it anyway. I felt someone had to be the grown-up. Dad never listened; he was stubborn and refused to take advice, just as he refused support from the social workers.

"You're too gobby, you have far too much to say," he complained, which always struck me as odd, because I felt I didn't speak enough. Though he was handy with his fists, Dad didn't scare me. If anything, I pitied him. When his temper boiled over, I always thought of Mum, weeping quietly on her mattress, and conversely, I took my strength from her.

2

BECAUSE MUM spent so much of her life in bed, I really looked forward to those three or four days when she was awake. These were little bursts of happiness which I held close to my heart. If she was frenzied or unbalanced, I tried not to notice. She radiated energy and something which was not quite happiness, a euphoria or a mania maybe. But I made excuses for all of her behaviours, rewriting them into a more acceptable narrative. She was at once the centre of my world, but also oddly out of reach, like a satellite, transmitting fuzzy and intermittent messages.

I adored my mother, in spite of her flaws but also because of them. Each frailty made her who she was; each aspect was a piece of the jigsaw which made her almost whole. When she shone brightly, I was dazzled. But when she was sad, my heart was broken. I loved being near her, trailing her around the house, chatting in the way I imagined grown-ups did. But I was more of a therapist or a parent and, in that role, I kept my own problems to myself. I knew it was my job to be a good listener. Even her voice changed when she was feeling better; she sounded more alert, more mature, and less childlike.

"I feel so sick this morning," she told me. "I think I might be pregnant again."

She seemed pleased, and I didn't want to pour cold water on her excitement by pointing out the practicalities. Another day, she said, "We owe a fortune to that London lot. We're going to get trouble tonight. Bet you they put the windows in again like last time."

A hard bubble of fear formed at the back of my throat. But at the same time, I was proud she had confided in me first. I felt special that I was chosen to carry her secrets, and I hoped it was a sign she loved me. The realisation was like a warm blanket over my shoulders, like melted chocolate oozing down my throat.

When Mum was happy, it was impossible not to be swept up in foamy waves of enthusiasm. She'd vanish late at night on a spontaneous trip to Asda, returning in the early hours with absolutely no food, but carrier bags bursting with trinkets and gifts. Each time, she brought me back a new teddy and my gifts sat proudly in a line on the top bunkbed. My favourite was Bedtime Bear, a blue Care Bear.

Other nights, she'd go out rooting through skips outside the big shops, bringing home new, or nearly new, clothes and shoes for us. As the eldest, I had first choice, but I divided everything out between us all, so it was fair. A t-shirt and a hair band for one sister and a dressing gown for another.

They weren't really the kind of clothes I wanted. Often the jeans were too baggy, or the trainers pinched at the toes. Or worse, Mum would bring home mini-skirts and high heels, clothes I might like to play dressing up in, but not to wear outside the house. She couldn't see why I didn't want to show them off at school. Again, it was another example of me being the adult, me being the sensible one, old, by necessity, before my time.

"Oh Tar, you'd look great in this," she'd giggle, holding up a leather-look mini-skirt and a spangly boob-tube.

"No Mum," I said firmly. "I'm way too young."

Sometimes, the clothes were ripped or stained, and they all carried the fetid smell of the skip, which was worse even than the smell of weed. But they were all I had and besides, they had come from my mother, which meant everything to me. The two sides of Mum were literally diametrical and there was no crossover between. Asleep, she might as well have been in a coma. But awake, she buzzed like an electric fence.

She had boundless energy and reminded me of a glass of bubbly lemonade, spilling over the rim when it was poured too quickly. My mother, at her best, was effervescent, full of fizz and vigour. She loved to clean and went through the whole house like a whirlwind, throwing Shake n Vac indiscriminately all over the floors, even though we had hardly any carpets left. As she dusted and polished, she sang her favourite songs by The Carpenters at the top of her voice and added in her own comical adaptations.

"I'm on Top of the World," she sang, "Looking down on this hoover!"

She could be so funny, and though I laughed at her jokes, it was enough for me just to see her smiling. Cleaning, I would later realise, gave her a control she didn't have over the other areas of her life. At times, inevitably, it tipped over into obsession. Once she spotted a stain on a carpet, so she pulled the whole thing up and threw it into the front garden in disgust.

Another time, she burned sausages in the frying pan and so the lot went in the bin. We had no frying pan for months afterwards. She would target certain items or rooms for a surgical clean, whilst turning a blind eye to the bin bags, the skip hauls and the drugs which cluttered our home. When Mum was sleeping, the clutter slipped quickly into squalor. When she was on one of her missions, the house was clinically clean, but it was not tidy. One morning, I woke to the sound of a whining drill and found Mum engrossed in an unspecified DIY project in the kitchen.

"Mum, I need to make breakfast so we can all get to school," I said.

"Not today," she called back cheerfully. "I've got big ideas for this kitchen."

When we came home later that day, she was still enthusiastically drilling. Another time, she ripped out the fireplace in the living room without being able to tell us why. After that, she pulled up the floorboards in the bathroom. But before she could finish any of these tasks, the energy drained from her as though someone had popped a balloon.

I could almost see her wilting and folding and she went from sky-high to flatlining in a matter of moments. She flopped back into bed, unable to resist the magnetic pull of the duvet, so immobile she might as well have been glued to the mattress. Hiding under the covers was not so much about sleep but more about retreating from the pain of her reality. And so, as she began another three-week stretch of withdrawal, her DIY projects were abandoned. She never finished a single one, and the holes in our walls and floors simply became a physical manifestation of the chaos and disorder inside her head.

Mum was always trying to make actual changes which, subconsciously, she hoped would help soothe her mental anguish. But nothing worked. All her efforts, like her shopping and her cleaning, were short-term, unplanned and ultimately unsuccessful. In the end, I think each failed mission added to her feelings of despair and worthlessness. I stuffed the redundant drill holes with old carrier bags, and I helped prop the fireplace up against the wall. On my way to the sink, I learned to step over the gaping hole in the bathroom, which served as a daily reminder of the gaping wound inside my mother.

One morning as I cleaned my teeth, I stepped backwards without thinking and I fell through the hole. I bruised my legs but was lucky not to fall right through to the kitchen below. It was the kind of thing me and Mum would have laughed about, but that morning, she was out cold on the mattress, and I knew better than to disturb her. Laughing on my own just wasn't much fun. At weekends, if Mum was up and about, we loved watching TV together. Her favourite show, *Blind Date*, was often a family affair, with Dad and the little ones all huddled together on our big brown sofa. This was another small sliver of normality, and I grasped the lie gratefully. But whilst everyone else was watching TV, my eyes were fixed firmly on my mother. I could predict her moods perfectly, and just as a parent can sense if their child is troubled or upset, I could sense that in my mother. I had a radar which detected each change of emotion. The transformation was subtle, but I knew her face as well as I knew my own. At the first suggestion of a shadow passing across her features, or a small sign that her mood was dipping, I'd stand up and do a goofy Charleston dance to make her laugh. Or I might sing songs by The Carpenters or The Pet Shop Boys.

'West End Girls!' I sang, twirling around, trying to catch her attention as she slumped back, glassy-eyed, on the sofa.

I did anything to make her smile, to keep her with me, just that little bit longer. But it was like holding a torrent of water behind a leaking dam or trying to prevent the daylight from slipping away each evening. I did my best to keep the darkness out. But somehow, it crept in with cold fingers, and as the *Blind Date* credits rolled, the shutters came down over my mother's eyes. She lay down on the mattress beside us; lost to us and lost to herself. I knew it could be days, maybe weeks, before she got up again. But that didn't stop Dad trying to rouse her. Sometimes he taunted her just to be cruel, other times, usually in the mornings, he took the stress of the school-run out on her. Furious at being under pressure himself, he would erupt, flipping her mattress so that she landed with a thump on the hard floor.

"Get up and see to these kids!" he yelled. "You're the one who wanted them all, not me!"

I could not stand by and see Mum hurt; it was like watching my own child suffer. No matter who was at fault, I was on her side, instinctively. I ran at Dad with my small fists bunched, my face screwed up in angry defiance.

"Leave her alone!" I yelled. "You're a big bully! Just leave her!"

I was regularly woken in the night to the sound of them fighting. In the morning, Mum would have bruises and patches of hair missing. Once, from the top of the stairs, I saw him beating her in the hallway. I grabbed a gas canister, which was the nearest object, and threw it at Dad. As it bounced down the stairs, Mum seized her chance to get away, but then he came for me instead. I had to run for my life and when he caught me, hiding behind the bathroom door, he gave me a crack across my face.

"You're just a gobby kid," he told me. "Don't get involved with me and your mum."

But I was not easily bullied, and he knew that.

"I'll always stand up for Mum," I retorted. "It's not right. You shouldn't hit her."

Another time, Mum asked me to stay off school to look after her. When Dad found out that night, he lost his temper. He had never before been concerned about me playing truant and I think it more likely he was just looking for a row. When he started throwing punches at Mum, I flew in, yelling at him to stop. Dad spun around and caught me full in the face. My nose erupted, spraying blood everywhere, and I staggered backwards, dizzy with shock.

"You broke my nose," I gasped, the blood gurgling at the back of my throat.

Dad was unrepentant.

"You shouldn't stick it in then! You will never amount to anything if you keep interfering!"

"But I am something!" I shouted. "I am!"

Even though I was covered in blood and pinching my nose, I had to have the last word. Eventually, I went to A&E to stop the bleeding, and doctors told me I had suffered a deviated septum. In addition to the cosmetic damage, I couldn't breathe properly either. Even then, Dad was not sorry. He and his friend nicknamed me 'Budgie' because of the bend in my nose where it had been broken and their barbs hurt me more than the injury itself. Those small cruelties were the worst. Why did Dad hate me? Why did he hit me? Was it because I was so outspoken, and I always took Mum's side over his? Or was it something more than that? Despite my bravado, his rejection stung. I felt like a helpless little ladybug, trapped under his big boot. But even then, I was not beaten. I shook my small fist and refused to be flattened.

Dad was mentally abusive to Mum too. She had once been a stunning woman with long dark hair and bright blue eyes. She had a wacky sense of style and would think nothing of nipping to the shop in July in a pair of winter boots and a fur coat. But over time, drugs had ravaged her inside and out. She was gaunt, almost skeletal, and though she was 5ft 7ins she could easily fit into aged nine to 10 children's clothes. As with most things, she cared less and less about her appearance as the years went by. Her hair was thinning, and she had lost nearly all of her teeth. Dad teased her whenever she smiled and cruelly nicknamed her: 'Gummy'. Mum always laughed it off with a quip of her own, but I saw the tears glistening in her eyes, her cheeks flushed with humiliation, and my hostility towards Dad cut deeper still. It was years before she could bring herself to attend an appointment with the dentist, but the new dentures didn't fit properly, they were far too big, and Dad made neighing noises, like a horse, whenever she wore them.

"Who will want me, looking like this?" she asked me dismally, as she spat the dentures into the sink.

To me, my mother was beautiful. I didn't understand why she couldn't see it. But her self-esteem was at rock bottom, and it had been that way for as long as I could remember. She took drugs to blot out her trauma but ultimately, predictably, they made her feel even worse than before. With each meltdown, with each fight with Dad, her dignity was further shredded. The last scraps ended up with the rubbish in the bin-bags which littered our garden. There were short periods, usually when she was pregnant, when she tried to reduce her drug intake. But then, Dad found something else to poke fun at. Without the amphetamines to keep her skinny, or due to a pregnancy, she began gaining weight.

"Fatty!" he laughed. "Look at the size of your belly."

The jibes only drove her back to drugs; to a place she felt safe, or rather, she felt nothing at all. Mum's relationship with amphetamines was pretty similar to her relationship with my father. In both cases, it was toxic, and they couldn't live with or without each other. It was so frustrating, knowing what was best for her but knowing also she would not change her ways. It was like parenting a difficult toddler, yet I was only a small child myself. Dad made Mum so miserable at times, yet I don't think she ever had the strength to consider leaving him permanently. Though she did have at least one brief affair, when she roped me in as an accomplice. I was very torn; I knew it was wrong, but Dad did not value her, and I believed she deserved better.

"You and me are going out today," she told me with a wink. "Don't tell anyone, especially not your dad."

I could never refuse my mother anything. Besides, I loved the idea of us spending time, just the two of us, and going off on a secret mission which nobody else knew about. She and I left the house together early one evening, which was, in itself, very unusual. She palmed my father off with a half-baked story about a trip to Asda, and I nodded my agreement. Further up the street we were collected by a man in a car who drove us to a wooded area nearby. My first thought was that he smelled strongly of aftershave, and not of weed, which I was used to. In the woods, he and Mum left me in the car whilst they went off somewhere together. I was too young to understand exactly what was happening, but I realised she was up to no good. I was frightened on my own, in a strange car, as darkness fell, but I didn't want to spoil Mum's fun and so I said nothing when she finally showed up. She swore me to secrecy afterwards but days later, Dad found out somehow and exploded with rage, blaming me for Mum's infidelity.

"You think you know it all!" he yelled.

He gave me a resounding smack across the face for my betrayal. Again, I wondered why everything was my fault and why he loathed me so much. In later years, I would question whether perhaps I was the result of an affair, and I was not his biological child. It's a dilemma which haunts me even now, and I will probably never know the truth. But even as I bathed my stinging cheeks after his slap, I couldn't find it in my heart to hate him back. He had his own issues, his own sadness.

As with Mum, the drugs had eaten away at his mind, and I made excuses for them both. His appearance, like Mum's, was ruined. As a young man, he looked just like Jay Kay, the singer from Jamiroquai; small, wiry and with bright eyes. But he had become skinny and scraggy, as though the drugs were slowly stripping the flesh from his bones. He seemed to have too much skin, and it hung in redundant folds around his eyes and mouth. There was a dullness in his expression, and even when his fists were flying, he seemed somehow defeated and crushed. There was a small part of me that always felt sorry for him, despite his cruelty.

Dad's violence was not our biggest problem. My parents were well-known as drug dealers as well as addicts and often they got on the wrong side of the bigger dealers, of disgruntled customers, and of the police. We lived in fear of a London gang who turned up without warning, often in the middle of the night, looking for money. My parents had wads of cash lying around, but it was never there for long, and never there when it was needed. I swallowed my own terror for the sake of the younger ones and tried to make those raids into an entertaining game, holding a slumber party in a makeshift tent in the bunkbeds. But there was nothing amusing about violent criminals smashing up our home and threatening to do the same to our faces.

One afternoon in the school holidays, I went with my younger sister to a local children's disco. After it finished, we set off on the short walk home and I was horrified to see Mum coming down the hill towards us, her face splattered in blood.

"Tar, they're still in the house!" she yelled.

I broke into a run, with no idea of what I was facing or what I would do. But the little ones were in there, defenceless, and I had to protect them. I found two men in the living room, huge hulks, and I ran at the first one, my heart racing with fear.

"Why are you hurting my Mum?" I shouted. "Leave my family alone."

He picked me up one-handed and threw me without a word into a cheese plant in the corner. I might as well have been an empty paper bag. Mum was close behind me and, as she screamed, he produced a gun from his pocket and aimed it towards her. My heart was already pounding and now it threatened to burst right through my rib cage. I'd no idea if it was a real gun but the fear was real enough.

"Don't hurt her," I pleaded, but I am not sure the words ever left my mouth.

"Just hand it over," he snarled, pushing the gun into Mum's head.

Dad had already fled, taking with him whatever cash or drugs they had come for. I can't remember how Mum persuaded them to leave us alone; maybe they just saw us for what we were; a terrified, defenceless mother and child, chewed up and spat out by life. But I do remember the taste of fear, cold and oddly metallic in my mouth, as though there was a gun to my head too. Mum consoled herself with a few pills after they'd gone. But as the house fell silent again, I found I could not stop shaking. I knew they'd be back soon.

At that moment, I needed an arm around me, a cuddle, a reassurance that we were all alright. But my mother did not give out affection; she only accepted it. I found her curled up on the floor, and I wrapped my arms around her shoulders and kissed her cheek. She repaid me with a look, and there was such love in her eyes, that I knew this was the best she could do.

"I'm sorry, I'm not good enough," she mumbled.

And yet, I idolised her. She would always be good enough for me.

In addition to strangers smashing our door down, there were plenty of strangers inviting themselves in, at all hours of the day and night. It was not unusual for me to cross the landing to the bathroom at night and see two or three adults loitering in our hallway. One evening, I went downstairs to get a glass of water for my little sister, and I was suddenly uncomfortable in my Minnie Mouse nightie as I squeezed past a line of men in our kitchen. I heard a whispered comment, a stifled laugh, and a sickly fear spread through me. I felt their eyes on me as I filled the glass and made my way back past them. I knew something was wrong here, something distasteful and warped, but I didn't know what it was. Instinctively, I got into the habit of clamping my hand over my private parts as I ran up and down the stairs, as though that would somehow protect me.

As a small child, aged four or five, I had always made eye contact with the strangers. I purposely started a conversation, asking their names and telling them mine. I thought, if we became friends, that they would never hurt me and I would be safe. By the time I was eight or nine, I had sadly wised up. I had seen too many fights, and heard too many windows smashed, to believe that any of these strangers could be my friends. I didn't even look at the people who came into our home. And yet, I could feel them looking at me, their eyes boring right through me in my flimsy nightie.

Even without violence, it was scary to have people drifting in and out of our home, as though it was a public place. I might as well have been sleeping in a bus shelter and sometimes, I think I'd have been safer there. To the left of our hallway was a door to a small shed with a fridge freezer inside and, when the black bin bags started to take over the living room, we threw them in there. My parents also allowed heroin addicts to jack up in the shed. I had to step over used needles on the floor in the same way that other kids stepped over stray Lego bricks. Once, I went into the shed for milk from the fridge and I spotted a trail of blood spattered in a bright red line across the freezer door and the wall. Nobody else seemed remotely concerned by it. I couldn't work out how my mother could spend three days cleaning the house and yet was content to have a stranger's blood squirted all over her fridge. I found a pan scourer, ran a bucket of hot water, and scrubbed it clean. I felt simultaneously far too young for the task and yet impossibly old and weary.

Interspersed with the attacks from the dealers and the disgruntled customers were the police raids. Sometimes, it was hard to tell them all apart. I lay in bed, stiff with terror, as officers banged the door down, arresting one of my parents, usually Mum, because Dad had scarpered. One of Dad's favourite tricks was to hide his drugs inside the babies' nappies. Either he believed, foolishly, that the police would not look there or, more likely, he accepted they might be searched but he would prefer that a total stranger removed his child's nappy, than risk being caught with drugs himself. He was willing to sacrifice his own children, again and again, to save himself. When the police came, I was ripped in two with split loyalties; I knew what my parents were doing was wrong and my father's behaviour was deplorable. From a young age, I had an inbuilt moral code, a clear sense of what was right. Yet I was fiercely and necessarily loyal. I would never have spoken to the police, just as I could not confide in a teacher or a social worker. My pain was my own. And yet, that sense of isolation made me tougher and stronger. I had nobody else to rely on and so I learned to trust only myself.

3

GOING BACK as far as I can remember, I was a regular visitor at my grandparents' house. My mother's parents, Mark and Carol, lived just a five-minute walk away. Their home was different in every way to ours and it was an oasis of safety and stability for me. A semi-detached on a quiet road, it was both peaceful and calm.

There were carpets on the floors and there was food in the cupboards. There was no stash of drugs, no strangers dropping by and no raiders banging down the front door. The little front lawn was regularly mowed and there were bright bedding plants nodding in welcome along the borders. Their home was low-key, run of the mill and perfectly normal. And so, I loved it there.

In the tranquillity of the empty rooms, I had the chance to collect my thoughts and recharge, ready for my return to the swirling maelstrom of chaos at home. My grandparents were huge Elvis fans, and every room was adorned with photos and paintings of the singer. They even had an Elvis clock with Elvis' legs swinging wildly on the hour. There was a stack of Elvis music and even as a toddler, I learned the words so I could sing along too.

'Everybody let's rock, Everybody in the whole cell block...'

My grandfather, or Grampy as I knew him, would twirl me around and lift me high in the air at the end of the song.

"Sure, you're a fantastic dancer, Tara, just like your Mum."

Grampy was not a tall man, but he was stocky. He had short grey hair, thick grey stubble on his cheeks, and he wore glasses. He was originally from Ireland and had, he told us proudly, served in the military as a young man. Sometimes, he'd lift me onto his knee and show me photos in his army uniform.

"That photo was taken in Congo," he told me. "I shot ten men there. I was a hero when I returned home to Ireland. I had a different woman every night; everyone loved me."

"Why did you leave Ireland, Grampy?" I asked, confused by his reference to women.

"We don't talk about that," he replied, pursing his lips.

Grampy had an air of quiet authority about him and when he spoke, he expected people to take notice. Everyone locally knew and respected him. He was charming and smiley, always ready with a joke or a funny comment. My mother was similar in some ways; on her good days, she could be very amusing, the way she tore through the house with the hoover like a whirlwind, or those nights when she arrived home from Asda with bundles of treats and her eyes dancing with delight. From the age of four, I visited Grampy on my own most weekends. Mum didn't come with me because she was usually in bed. But Grampy seemed happy to call in and collect me, carrying me through the streets of Swindon on his shoulders. In those moments, I was 10 feet tall. I felt as though I mattered, as though someone had noticed me at last. I was a small princess, paraded through the streets on the shoulders of my hero. Better than that, Grampy took control, he shouldered responsibility, and so I didn't have to. The relief was wonderful. He made a point, also, of always taking my side. At home, I was used to being ignored, or worse, scoffed at. But when I told Grampy the other kids at school had been nasty, he took it very seriously.

"You tell me their names, I'll sort them out," he promised.

If I confided I needed a new pencil case, he'd take me to the shop, that same weekend, to buy one.

"Nothing but the best for my little Tara," he said. "You're my girl, you know that."

He was my saviour, the only family member I had who truly heard me when I spoke, who recognised not only that I was a child, but that he was the adult. If I told him I was hungry, which I usually was, he had a solution for that too. His cupboards were well-stocked, and it was sometimes bamboozling to have so much choice. Grampy had learned to cook in the army, and he was a great chef. He could rustle up a tasty sausage and mash, liver and onions or a shepherd's pie. They were good, home-cooked meals and comforting for a little girl who craved affection just as much as she craved food. Whilst Grampy was cooking, he taught me how to follow his recipes.

"Here, Tara, you peel these carrots whilst I slice the onions," he said. "We're such a good team."

He was, in many ways, the dependable father figure I so desperately lacked. Unlike at home where our whole existence teetered on a cliff edge, I found the organisation and stability here at Grampy's to be reassuring. A weekly shop, direct debits for bills, a regular bedtime; they were the things everyone else took for granted. But to me, it was like winning the lottery. After we'd eaten on a Saturday evening, Grampy took me to Blockbuster as a treat, and I was allowed to pick a video to watch before he took me home. I savoured those moments of deliberation, my eyes flitting from *Tom and Jerry* to *Cinderella* to *Chitty Chitty Bang Bang*. The cornucopia of choice was almost too mind-boggling. I enjoyed the films, but it wasn't so much the video itself that I appreciated, more that Grampy had made the effort to do something just for me. I wasn't used to being considered, never mind prioritised, and it was lovely. As we cuddled up on the sofa with the lights down low, Grampy would produce a box of Jaffa cakes or chocolate teacakes. He knew they were my favourites.

"One for each hand," he smiled, his Irish accent no more than a distant suggestion.

Guiltily, as the final credits rolled, I began to think once again about home. I worried about leaving my siblings whilst I was away and felt inexplicably guilty that I had enjoyed something without them. Yet I had to admit, the freedom was lovely. For a few short hours, with Grampy, I felt I had permission to be a little girl again. I could almost be myself. The never-ending worries which plagued me at home were, for a time at least, suspended somewhere outside our front door.

After I started at primary school, my weekend visits continued. I looked forward so much to seeing Grampy; being hoisted onto his shoulders and carried through the streets, just like any other little girl. That was all I wanted. I didn't dream of fairytale castles or story-book princesses or untold riches. I was grateful simply for those brief snapshots of normality offered by my visits.

The gentle routine of cooking a meal, walking to Blockbuster, and sharing a packet of Jaffa cakes on the sofa, was therapy for my injured heart. After the film finished, we walked home and I was plunged right back into the bedlam of my parents screeching and fighting, of leering strangers, of police raids, of playtimes hidden in the school toilets, fearfully watching the clock. What was happening at home? Was everyone safe? Was my mother still alive? My visit to Grampy's was instantly forgotten as the stress of my home life spread like a rash over me. In the mornings, I couldn't wait to get out of the house and yet, as soon as I escaped, I was desperate to go back. Perversely, I felt like a mother who had left her children alone all day and was waiting for an accident to happen.

"Tara, whatever's the matter?" my teacher asked, as I gulped back tears in the classroom.

"Nothing, Miss," I lied. "I had something in my eye."

I was just a small child and yet my insecurities were piled up like the black bin bags in our garden. My whole existence felt brittle, inside and out, as though I might snap at any moment.

I was around five years old when, one night, I woke to hear Mum sobbing. Quietly, I climbed down the ladder of the bunk bed and went into the bathroom to soak a cold flannel, before making my way down to the living room. She was sitting on the mattress, hunched over, with her head in her hands. With each sob, her bony shoulders rose and fell and her ribcage flared. It was as though her whole body was consumed by sorrow. My own tears flowed in sympathy even though I didn't know what was wrong.

"Mum," I said gently. "Shh, I'm here now."

I wiped her forehead and her hands with my flannel, but she seemed to cry even harder.

"What's the matter?" I whispered, climbing onto the mattress beside her.

"Everything is the matter with me," she replied, her voice threaded with bitterness. "Do you know why I am like this, Tara? Do you know why I'm such a mess?"

There was something in her tone which made me keep quiet.

"You should ask Grampy," she stuttered eventually. "See

what he says. See if admits to abusing me. His own daughter. That's what happened, Tara. Grampy sexually abused me when I was a little girl. He raped me. And that's why I'm like this."

There was a small part of me that welcomed the confidence from my mother, as always. She was relying on me and that meant she loved me. But the bigger part of me was confused and overwhelmed. I didn't understand at all what she was saying. I sensed only that something bad had happened. Something terrible. Grampy, I knew, was a kind and friendly man. I'd never even seen him lose his temper. There had to be some mistake. And yet, I hated to see Mum so distressed. I didn't know what to do.

"Go back to bed," she said abruptly. "I'll be okay. You've got school tomorrow."

She didn't talk about it the next day and I never asked. That was how it was in our family; layer upon layer of secrets, incidents we must never recount, memories we must never repeat. And so, I added Mum's latest disclosure to the list and pushed it to the back of my mind.

When I was six years old, it was decided I would spend each weekend with Grampy, going on Thursday evenings after school and returning on Sunday afternoons. The fizz of excitement I felt at escaping the disarray at home was followed by a twinge of regret. What about my siblings? What about my mother? How would they manage without me?

"I just need to tuck the little ones into bed before I come with you," I told Grampy, that first Thursday.

"Don't you worry," Grampy said, as he lifted me onto his shoulders. "Sure, they'll be fine. Your dad is here. And we're only just up the road if they need us."

Off we went, me with one arm around Grampy's neck and the other clutching my blue Care Bear. Nobody waved goodbye, nobody even noticed I had gone. There was a rueful sort of bliss in knowing I was leaving behind all my problems and responsibilities. I hated leaving everyone, but I relished it too. Grampy already had a casserole in the oven, and I was starving. My mother had failed to sign the free school meals form again and so apart from a Twix from Miss Bond, I'd had nothing to eat all day.

After our casserole, I had a bubbly bath, all to myself, before Grampy tucked me up in the big double bed upstairs. I was used to sharing; squeezing up against the bath wall so the little ones could sit beside me and squashing up in bed, with a tiny scrap of pillow, so there was space for a little one and the teddies too. I had nothing of my own. All our clothes, shoes, food, toys, were shared. So this was a slightly strange experience, lying in a large double bed with so much space and silence stretching out around me. The bedroom was so big that there was another bed, a single, over by the window, next to a wardrobe and a chest of drawers. The wallpaper was floral and old-fashioned, and the beige curtains were made from a heavy silk. The double bed where I slept was layered with crisp sheets and soft blankets. On top of an ivory bedspread, plump white pillows completed the picture. This was, I told myself, a bed fit for a fairytale princess.

"This is the most comfortable bed in the world," I said, snuggling into my pillow. "I love it here, Grampy."

After school the next day, he took me to Blockbuster.

"You can choose a film, and we'll stay up late tonight," he smiled. "Anything for my girl."

We watched *Snow White* together, and then Grampy got up from his chair, and I heard the sharp snap of a ring-pull as he opened a can of lager in the kitchen. When he came back, he began sorting through the pile of videos which were stored under the TV unit. Most were labelled: 'Elvis On Tour', 'Best of Elvis' or 'Coronation Street – Monday.' Grampy picked up a blank cassette, slotted it into the player, and settled back into his chair with an almost inaudible grunt. The film began and I was half transfixed, half repulsed, as an image of three naked adults appeared on the screen. I could not bear to look. Yet I could not bear to look away.

"What do you think of it?" Grampy asked casually slurping his lager, as though we were watching another Disney classic.

I was never usually lost for words, but they dried in my throat. I had no idea what I was seeing. But instinctively, I felt it was not right. Just as it was wrong for my parents to take drugs, just as it was wrong to beat children, this was also wrong. Yet more so. Much more. As the video played on, I concentrated on watching Grampy, and not the television. As with Mum, when she was watching *Blind Date*, I studied his face for clues, but I was bewildered. He stared without speaking at the screen until it was over. And then he said softly, "You are so like your mum Tara. You're a special child."

I was even more confused. In the days afterwards, I turned his words over and over in my mind and examined them. I had been so sure the video was wrong. But perhaps it was a treat, a reward of some sort? Surely being compared to my mother was a compliment, and with that thought I swelled with pride. I was special, he had told me so himself. I was chosen. Maybe, I reasoned, watching the video with Grampy was a sign that I was cherished and valued. Being loved was the greatest gift I could think of, and the one I longed for the most. The next weekend when I visited Grampy, the video was already playing when I walked into the living room after dinner. Again, I tried not to watch, but even the noises made my stomach turn.

"Do you like it?" Grampy asked, a can of lager in his hand. "Do you?"

I avoided his gaze. I knew I was expected to say yes. But much as I wanted to be loved, much as I wanted to be special, much as I wanted to please him, I could not ignore my gut feeling. An inner steeliness pushed its way to the surface as I said, "No, I don't."

I worried Grampy might be annoyed, but he said nothing. I stepped back, ready to leave the room, but he snapped, "Sit down. Do as I tell you."

His voice was spiky and, with a shiver, I realised it would not be a good idea to push him too far. When the film had finished, he slid the tape back into the cardboard case and stacked it up with the others: 'Elvis, The King', 'Elvis on Tour', 'Elvis 1972'. The nameless tape slotted in amongst the others like an evil imposter.

"Now," Grampy said. "How about a chocolate teacake for my girl?"

Again, I was wrong-footed. Why would he make me watch those disgusting films but then give me my favourite treat? Was Grampy nasty or nice? Surely, he could not be both. The films became a regular fixture in my weekend stays and though I dreaded having to watch them, I still looked forward to my visits. They were, after all, an escape – my only escape – from the pandemonium at home. The films slowly and insidiously became a part of our routine. And yet at the same time, the process was terrifyingly quick. In those first few moments of that first video, Grampy went from someone I trusted and loved, to someone I feared and barely knew. Like the two sides of my mother, there was no common ground between his two distinct selves.

One Friday evening, he gave me a pound coin to spend in the corner shop. When we got back, he ran me a bath and told me to get undressed. I was more than capable of getting myself into bed; at home, I was used to looking after the little ones as well as myself. I was busy washing my knees, surrounded by bubbles, when the bathroom door opened and

Grampy walked in. He locked the door with a click and there was a finality to the sound which made my heart contract.

"Give me the flannel," he said, without meeting my eye.

He began by washing my legs but soon worked his way higher until he reached my private parts. I saw the flannel floating in the suds and realised he now was using his hands.

"Grampy!" I gasped suddenly. "Please stop. That hurts!"

"Be quiet, Tara, that's my girl," he replied, his voice no more than a whisper.

For what felt like an age, I said nothing, holding my breath and willing it to be over. The bathroom window was open and outside, I could hear the birds chirping. All at once I was so grateful. It seemed as though they were singing just for me. Closing my eyes, I focussed firmly on the bird song, and, at that moment, I felt myself lifted, out of the bath, through the narrow window, and into the clear, warm evening air. Off I flew, with the little birds chittering beside me, ushering me along. I was free. Truly free. Grampy stood up when it was over and I flew back inside, into my own body and into the lukewarm bath water.

"You are so like your mother," Grampy smiled, as he held out the towel for me.

Again, I was blindsided. Was this, like those awful films, supposed to be some sort of gift or reward for me? Had I been selected because Grampy loved me so much? This was, after all, the focus and attention I had always yearned for. How could it be a bad thing? Grampy seemed happy and calm and there was no sign of any upset or anger. Was this his way of showing that he loved me, or that he hated me?

I wondered whether I'd been chosen because of my likeness to my mother and whether this was why Grampy invited me here every weekend. I was closer to the sickening truth than I could ever have imagined, but aged six, I was clutching at broken straws, trying to make sense of an incident which had left me reeling. Was it because I myself was a miniature parent, someone who took on the responsibility of others? I was the one in charge of looking after the others, of fixing their problems and healing their pain. Maybe this was all part of the package, and it was just another depressing aspect of being an adult. And if this was completely normal, perhaps it was happening in other homes also. I already knew my own home was dysfunctional in the extreme, so I could not look to my parents to set an example. And neither, when I returned home, could I bring myself to confide in them.

They were so wrapped up in their own problems, so immersed in their own self-pity, that they had no time for me. I resolved, instead, to push the memories of what had happened in the bathroom to the very back of my memory, to the dusty corners where I would never come across them again. Hopefully, on my next visit, Grampy would let me bath myself. In the meantime, I settled into a new role of pretending that my grandfather was a nice old man who bought me chocolate teacakes and Jaffa cakes, who gave me pound coins to spend in the corner shop, and took me to

Blockbuster. The rest, I blocked out. But the shreds of that atrocious memory lay embedded in my soul like shards of glass. I could not eradicate them all. Thursday evening seemed to come around more quickly that week and, when Grampy arrived to collect me, fear bloomed in me like fungus. I did not want to go with him, but neither did I want to stay at home.

"Come on, Tara," he smiled, hoisting me onto his shoulders.

Whilst I was running my bath that same evening, I heard the snap of a ring-pull downstairs as Grampy opened his can of lager. My insides, already twisting, now knotted even tighter. Next, I heard his footsteps on the stairs, each one bringing him perilously nearer to me.

"There's my girl," he smiled, pushing his head around the door.

The bathroom lock snapped suddenly shut like a mousetrap. I felt so vulnerable. I might as well have been lying on a giant chopping board with a huge cleaver hanging over me. As the blade came down towards me, I felt Grampy's hands on my skin. I closed my eyes, listened for the bird song, and off I flew. I had known they would not let me down; my friends, the birds. When I landed back in the bath, I saw a thin streak of blood in the water.

"Come on Tara, that water will be going cold," Grampy said, offering his hand as I climbed out of the bath. "Now, do you remember what happened to your Mum?"

Despite the smile, there was a malevolence in his tone, a suggestion that I would not want to end up like her. And he was right; I didn't want to spend my days sleeping, crying and wailing. Much as I adored my mother, and I loved the comparisons, I did not want to live my life as she did hers. I did not at first understand why he would link Mum's depression with what had happened in the bathroom. But slowly, like moths, the memory of her words fluttered back to me, brushing against my face in my darkness.

"Grampy sexually abused me when I was a little girl. He raped me. That's why I'm like this."

Was this sexual abuse? Was this the same thing that had happened to Mum? I did not know. But the prospect of metamorphosing into my mother; sleeping and sweating on a bare mattress, taking daily beatings, her eyes lighting up only when she spotted her next pill, filled me top to toe with pure, liquid dread.

"No," I said firmly to myself. "No, that can't happen."

And yet, there was no way out of visiting Grampy. I was too afraid to complain and anyway, nobody would have listened.

One weekday evening, as I was bathing the little ones at home, I had a sudden, urgent flashback to Grampy's bathroom. I saw again his slippery hands darting like fish through the water. I felt again the searing, sickening, pain. The images shot through me like poison and, as I stumbled out onto the landing, I broke down sobbing. In that moment, I desperately needed to confide in someone. Mum was downstairs, and I could hear the TV in the background, so I knew she was awake. I went into the living room, still crying, and huddled next to her. She glanced at me but said nothing, and so I cried even more loudly, forcing out my sobs so that she would have no option but to ask me what was wrong. That was all I needed, for my mother to formulate that single sentence and show that she cared.

Just ask me, Mum. Please, just ask.

But as the minutes ticked by and I continued to cry, my mother said nothing. Eventually, a little voice drifted down the stairs:

"Tara! Help me squeeze the toothpaste on my brush!"

"Go on," Mum said, nodding at the door. "They're calling for you."

If any was needed, this was cold, hard confirmation that my mother was not there for me.

4

THE WEEKDAYS unravelled quickly into weekends, and I did not know which I dreaded the most. The sexual abuse by my grandfather continued alongside the mental and physical abuse at home. How could these two houses, these two alternate versions of hell, be my only choices in life? I was not forced to visit Grampy at weekends, but I did not need to be. As a little child, starved of love, I was prepared to put up with anything, anything at all. My heart breaks when I think of how alone I was, trapped, quite literally, between the devil and the deep blue sea. And paradoxically, no matter how desperately I wished to escape, I could never have left my mother and my siblings. I was manacled to my family by heavy chains of love and shame. There was no way out.

My visits to Grampy settled into a pattern, with the first few hours of every Thursday evening passing uneventfully. Grampy collected me, took me to his house, and we cooked our dinner together. Afterwards, we might go to Blockbuster to rent a film, or we'd look through old black and white photos from his albums. Sometimes, he became teary as he recounted stories from the past and the show of emotion never failed to pull at my heartstrings. The monster lurked beneath, but he hid it well. Looking back, I recognise that those manufactured displays were all part of an orchestrated plan of grooming. But as a little girl, I felt each and every one of his tears. Sitting on the sofa, with the photo albums open on our laps, he told me that his house was haunted. Like a spider, he pulled me into his web. As with my mother, I was flattered and proud that he chose to confide in me.

"Have you heard the voices?" he asked. "Can you feel the spirits, right beside us now?"

I was a vulnerable, suggestible child, and I wanted to believe in spirits. More than that, I wanted to believe my Grampy. Once, we were in the living room when a shutter door which led to the back room suddenly closed on its own. Instinctively, I moved closer to Grampy on the sofa.

"Don't worry my girl," he comforted. "You're safe with me."

The irony chokes me now. But back then, my fear of the ghosts added to my fear of the house and made me all the more reliant on Grampy. Perhaps that was all part of his plan. As I grew older, I became more interested in spirituality and again, Grampy's interests aligned with mine, or perhaps mine aligned with his. He was always one step ahead of me, and I had no idea that I was being controlled and manipulated. Even with the ghosts, those evenings watching a Blockbuster film or listening to Grampy's wartime exploits were happy enough. But the moment I heard the snap of that first can of lager, I knew I was in trouble. Grampy had a secret stash of cans behind a shelf in a kitchen cupboard, and as soon as he began drinking, he seemed to switch character. His Irish accent became more pronounced, to the point where it felt like an affectation. He sounded like a different man. His face hardened, his unseeing eyes like two small pebbles. He was sharp with me; impatient and unkind. He bore no resemblance to the other Grampy, the one I adored and who professed to adore me. Like my mother, he had two distinct and completely separate personalities. Both had Jekyll and Hyde characters, and I would later understand that one had been the trigger for the other. But as a small child, these different psyches were impossible to comprehend. Not only did I, aged seven, have to manage the adults in my life, but I also had to navigate their shifting moods and personalities. No wonder I was on edge all the time, always on the verge of the next disaster, of the next drama. With Grampy, I worked out that the first lager was a clear sign he was going to assault me. Once, I was so afraid when I heard that familiar snap of a can that I squeezed myself into the narrow space between the washing machine and a kitchen cupboard. It was hopeless; there was no door to hide me, and he spotted me easily.

"I'm sorry Grampy," I muttered. "I was just playing hide and seek."

As he pulled me out, I had a fleeting insight into how my

mother felt, being flipped from her mattress by my father in the mornings. She did not have a safe space. And now, neither did I. Some evenings as he was drinking, Grampy forced me to watch pornography, instructing me to perform sex acts on myself and on him whilst he watched. I had no idea what I was doing, I knew only that I hated it. And by the time it was over, I hated myself. I was bewildered by his behaviour, and my own, and still no nearer to understanding whether the abuse was a symbol of love or loathing. I grew to dread bathtimes and the ominous click of the lock on the bathroom door.

Shivering in fear, I felt naked inside as well as out; it was as though he was hollowing me out, scraping away at my exposed soul. I am thankful, even now, to those little birds who flew to my rescue, carrying me off with them, away from my brutal reality and into fluffy white clouds of oblivion. The attacks in the bathroom were, and still are, very clear in my mind, stark in both detail and vulnerability. But other memories were blurry and indistinct. Uninvited, they flew through my mind like drones, and it was impossible to know where or when each image belonged.

Under Grampy's stairs was a cupboard where he kept toys. My favourites, as a small child, were a big red bus and a yellow teapot filled with tiny cups and saucers. Without many toys of my own at home, I'd spend hours pushing the bus up and down the hallway or stacking cups into the teapot. But one night after my bath, Grampy opened the door to the cupboard, and I was paralysed with fear; gripped head to toe by a nameless dread. I could not bear to even look at the toys, less still touch them. I did not know why I was so afraid, I could not remember an attack, but I was certain it had happened. Not knowing was almost worse, because instead of a scar, there was a great, gaping wound inside me.

On one level, the bus and the teapot were simply toys. On another, they were witness to unspeakable crimes. Sometimes, walking past the cupboard, I squeezed my eyes shut and tried to retrieve the lost memory. But other days, my courage wavered, and I pushed it deeper still.

When home time came, on Sunday afternoon, Grampy always switched effortlessly back into his alter-ego. His bag of Jaffa cakes and his cheery jokes no longer had me fooled, and yet there was nothing I could do with this new knowledge, nobody I could confide in. As he lifted me onto his shoulders and carried me outside, I felt weak with relief. The feeling of the wind on my face was confirmation that I was free, temporarily at least. But my elation did not last and by the time we arrived home, the problems quickly piled up again. I was pulled from one crisis to another and really, I did not know which form of abuse was worse. And anyway, I was still doubtful that this was in fact abuse. I didn't know what it was. When Grampy brought me home, I studied the way in which he spoke with my parents and to my confusion, they all seemed to get on so well. Grampy was critical of Dad behind his back.

"Good for nothing, no more than a layabout and a druggie," he'd say to others.

But to Dad's face, Grampy was all smiles. Both my parents seemed to like him. When Mum was awake, she seemed to light up and sparkle during his visits. She appeared to adore him; hanging onto his words and basking in the warm glow of his approval. That didn't match with the way I'd seen her cry and accuse him of the most despicable crimes. And when he left, she deteriorated visibly. She seemed to shrivel, as though he had taken her energy away with him. Once, as the front door closed behind him, she began wailing at the top of her voice and I presumed, logically, that she was sad to see him leave. This made no sense at all to me. If the abuse was wrong, why did my parents welcome Grampy into their home? And worse, why on earth did they send me to his? I wrestled with these questions; saying them out loud when I was locked in the school toilet, chasing them round and round my head like wasps. And yet still, I was no nearer to any answers. What was abuse and why was it acceptable in our flawed family? It did not help that my parents' general approach to morality was, at best, blurred. Some mornings, when I found Mum crying, she'd admit Dad had forced himself upon her the previous night.

"He made me have sex, Tar," she sobbed. "I'd no choice."

Other times, when they were bickering during the day, she'd tell me, "We haven't had sex today, that's why he's annoyed. I need to give it him and he'll calm down."

I grew up believing sex was a chore, like emptying the bins; unpleasant but essential to maintain an equilibrium. Conversely in our house, nobody actually emptied the bins. My parents never considered that these conversations were unsuitable for children, just as they never thought drug use around us was inappropriate. But even against a backdrop of appallingly loose morals, Grampy's abuse of me was dreadful, and my parents' complete denial of it even more so. I preferred to tell myself they didn't know about it. I wanted to believe that. But as I grew older, I could not help but match up what had happened to my mother with what was happening to me. And in darker moments, I suspected they were all in it together. I feared I was caught, like a butterfly in a net, in a depraved family cult.

5

AROUND THREE years after the abuse began, I overheard an argument between my parents, with my father annoyed that my mother was possibly pregnant again.

"How can you be?" he yelled. "You can't keep doing this. We can't look after the kids we already have!"

"It's not my fault," she yelled back. "You're the one who keeps making me have sex. I don't even want to do it."

"No. You don't want to do anything you lazy cow. That's your trouble."

And so it went on. As I listened, a kernel of worry germinated in my gut. I was beginning to figure out that the strangers on Grampy's horrible films were having sex, like my parents. So could I become pregnant, from watching pornography? Or maybe from the revolting things Grampy did with his hands when I was in the bath? I was nine years old, and the idea seemed perfectly plausible. The fear sprouted inside me and wrapped around my heart like poison ivy.

At school, locked in the toilet cubicle, I had something new to fret about. On top of all of my many other layers of anxiety, I now worried I was going to have a baby. Tears stung my eyes as I realised I would have to cope with yet another child. Already, I cared for my younger siblings. I could not manage a baby of my own as well. The horror sat at the forefront of my thoughts and dominated everything. I reminded myself how Mum screamed and sobbed when she gave birth in the upstairs bedroom. Would I have to go through that too? I remembered how she bought tests each time she thought she was pregnant and back at home, I hurried into the bathroom to check the cabinet but couldn't find any. Later that week, Mum came to the end of a mini-hibernation and was filled with her customary vitality.

"I'm going to Asda," she announced, late one evening.

"Can I come?" I asked.

It was a school night, but Mum had never been the sort to enforce bedtimes.

"Sure," she grinned.

I'd previously had an inkling that Mum did not pay for the treasures she brought home from Asda and as we wandered down the aisles, it was confirmed. I watched her dropping jewellery, socks and even a pair of slippers down the front of her coat. I was at once appalled and inspired. As we passed the chemist aisle, I reached out, grabbed a pregnancy test, and popped it into my pocket. We walked out soon afterwards, without a single challenge. Mum couldn't wait to distribute her haul amongst my siblings, but I was not interested in the bangles or the frilly ankle socks. The pregnancy test was burning a hole in my pocket. Upstairs, I read the instructions carefully and worked out it was best to do the test in the morning. I made sure I was in the bathroom before anyone else, and, avoiding the holes in the floorboards, I waited for what I felt was the inevitable positive result. The minutes ticked by and there were no lines at all on the test stick.

"Tara!" Dad shouted, hammering on the door. "Open up. I need the toilet."

I'd messed up the test. There was no other explanation. And so I was no nearer finding out whether or not I was pregnant. It was a heavy burden for a nine-year-old and I felt reduced, shorter and smaller, as though the pregnancy was already taking its toll physically. Miss Bond must have sensed my upset and called me over in the corridor. Though she was no longer my class teacher, she always caught up with me at breaktimes, inviting me into her office for a chat and a bar of chocolate.

"Is anything worrying you, Tara?" she asked kindly.

I shook my head. How could I begin to tell her that Grampy made me watch sex films and I thought I might be pregnant, but I had stolen a test, messed it up, and had no idea how to get hold of another one? I was just a child.

"You can tell me," she pressed. "I'd like to help."

But Dad's voice rang out in my head, each word striking my skull like a hammer blow.

Tell them nothing. Or they'll take you away.

No matter how much my worries were tearing me apart, I knew better than to share them with a stranger.

"I'm fine, Miss, thank you," I mumbled.

As always seemed to be the way, my problems were never resolved but simply shunted aside and forgotten when something even worse happened. And at Grampy's, the following weekend, that is exactly what happened. He had, without explanation, allowed me to bath on my own that Saturday evening. But as I was getting dried and into my Minnie Mouse nightie, I heard a snap downstairs as he opened a can and my heart plummeted. I knew what was coming. He appeared on the landing soon after and ushered me into the third bedroom, a spare room which was used for surplus clothes and furniture. There was no bed. I was allowed to play in there sometimes, but I couldn't remember ever being in there with Grampy. He stood, for a moment, and stared at me. The air crackled. I could almost taste the tension.

"Come here, Tara," he slurred.

My instinct was to run but my legs, suddenly heavy, were rooted to the ground. I was afraid to do as he said, yet I was equally afraid to disobey him. I opened my mouth to protest but the words dried in my throat, and nothing came out.

"Come here, my girl," he said.

He smiled but the eyes behind his glasses were cold and hard, his gaze fixed upon me like a snake with a small mouse. With one hand he unbuckled his trousers and with the other he grabbed a fistful of my long hair and yanked my head towards him. I saw the danger coming. Quick as a flash, I scurried to the corner at the back of my mind.

'Tomorrow will come,' I told myself. 'Tomorrow is not far away.'

From the safety of my secret room, I watched the attack in bursts, as though it was being beamed through a faulty stream on the TV. There were short reels of my head being forced up and down, accompanied by audio of Grampy, groaning and muttering, his accent strong and aggressive.

"My girl," he grunted. "Just like your mother."

The flashes continued: A gold watch on his wrist. The sour smell of lager on his breath. His tongue lolling slightly. His shirt sleeves rolled up. Always a shirt and smart trousers to fool the outside world.

'This will not last,' I reminded myself. 'Tomorrow will come.'

Grampy was out of breath when it was over. I could not help but gag at the vile taste in my mouth.

"Clean your teeth and get into bed," he muttered.

That night I was plagued by memories, not a full account of the attack, but distinct and dislocated clips, as confusing as they were disturbing. The stench stuck with me long after I had managed to push away the sounds and images. It was a fleshy, putrid smell which caught at the back of my throat and which I knew would haunt me for the rest of my life. But even then, even when the final fragments of my innocence were shattered, I made no objection to visiting him the following weekend.

My willingness to return to my abuser hurts me almost

as much as the abuse itself. I was so lost and lonely that I was prepared to undergo any amount of suffering in return for what I thought was love. And still, I was unsure whether my visits to Grampy were a punishment or a prize. Did my parents send me there because they hated me or because they wanted to reward me? Did Grampy like me or loathe me? I had no idea. But I no longer enjoyed my time with Grampy, and even during our trips to Blockbuster or our evenings cooking up a stew or a steak and kidney pie, there was a tension brewing like an ugly storm cloud overhead.

The house itself began to frighten me even more than Grampy. My own home, for all the chaos and depravity, was transparent. There was no attempt to paper over the problems and the smell of cannabis wafting down the street in warning was testament to that. But at Grampy's, the respectable veneer; the neat front lawn, the well-stocked kitchen, the smart shirt and trousers, was grossly at odds with the evil within. The house was light and clean, and yet it was shrouded in darkness and infected with disease. Nobody cared or noticed who came and went at my house. Yet Grampy's house dragged me in and did not let me leave. I imagined it like a great octopus with many long tentacles snatching me up and swallowing me whole.

The ghosts cackled and heckled from their hiding places. The walls creaked with sordid secrets and groaned with shame. Silent witnesses, like me, they were powerless to speak out. My family home was shaky, built on an emotional landmine. Like a house of cards, it was constantly under threat of collapse, just like its inhabitants. It was like a roller coaster ride, where I had to grip tightly onto the sides and hope not to fall off. But Grampy's home stood strong, solid and unassailable. I had once mistaken that strength as reassurance and comfort. Now, I saw it for what it was. Step inside, and it was a cesspit, a swamp, which threatened to close over my head and drown me.

As a child, I enjoyed my visits because the peace and quiet allowed me time to think and to make decisions. Now, I tried to avoid thinking at all costs. I did not want to dwell on what was happening to me. Instead, I pushed all the trauma aside, hiding it deep down inside myself in the forgotten rooms of my mind. I packed it away in different cubby holes and corridors inside my head. I was like a Matryoshka doll, with several different versions, each one hidden inside the next. I had to lock one part of my life away so that I could function in another. It was the only way.

I should have known, when I woke to the sound of my parents screaming and crockery smashing, that this day was going to be even worse than usual. Dad had flipped Mum off her mattress in a rage, and they'd had a fight. By the time I got the little ones downstairs ready for school, Dad had disappeared, taking the drugs with him. It was just another spat, but it meant I had to manage my mother, and my siblings, whilst getting everyone out of the door on time for school. Aged nine, I was responsible for the school run on my own and the responsibility clipped around me like a harness. In the kitchen, I was trying to make a jam sandwich for one sister, whilst fastening shoes for another, whilst looking around for a hairbrush to do our ponytails. Mum appeared at the door and snapped, "Keep the noise down, Tara. I'm trying to sleep!"

I never normally expected anything of my mother, but today, I was juggling too many jobs. It was like trying to catch running water in my hands.

"Why can't you help me?" I snapped back. "Why is everything up to me?"

Mum had never laid a finger on me but in that moment, she lunged towards me, squeezing her hands around my neck. I dropped the butter knife and screamed. Perhaps I blacked out, or I blocked it out. For in the next moment, Mum was draping a woolly scarf around my neck which was already red and stinging.

"I'm sorry, I'm sorry," she mumbled. "Keep this on at school. If anyone asks, keep quiet."

She pulled down the scarf to check on my bruising before I left, and then, she went back to bed. Even then, as my neck swelled, I felt such sympathy for her. I knew she had not meant to hurt me. She was misunderstood and lost. It was my role, as her daughter, to help with her demons and not punish her for them. Later, as I took my seat in class, my teacher asked me to remove my scarf.

"You don't need to wear that inside," she smiled.

Wide-eyed, I clutched it tightly, remembering Mum's instructions. I did not want to disobey her. But neither did I want to get into trouble at school.

"Tara," she said, holding out her hand.

Wordlessly, I handed over the scarf to reveal a ring of fingerprint bruises around my neck. The teacher frowned and took me into The Rainbow Room, an area dedicated to children who needed extra support. I'd been in there many times before. Today, Miss Bond was waiting.

"What happened to your neck, Tara?" she asked gently.

My eyes swam with tears as I stared at my shoes.

"I can help you, Tara," she pressed. "Please talk to me."

But I could not, dared not, reply. Over and over, I shook my head, twisting my hands together. One half of me screamed out silently for help. The other was determined to keep my secret as my parents' warnings sounded like an air raid siren in my mind. Miss Bond brought me a plastic cup of orange cordial and some custard creams, and I was kept in the Rainbow Room, long after the final bell rang. Finally, I was taken outside to where Dad was waiting. The moment we got into the street, he flew at me.

"We've had social workers round this afternoon," he hissed. "This is what happens when you blab, you gobby little cow."

Trudging home, with my neck sore and swollen, I felt so weary. I did not even bother to explain that I hadn't blabbed to anyone. It would have been pointless anyway. He would blame me regardless.

"You will go into care now, all of you," he finished, with a sour note of triumph.

His words sliced like blades through my skin. No matter how difficult life was, I was petrified of going into care. The thought of leaving my mother was unbearable. Mentally, I doubled-down on my resolution never to speak to anyone at all about my home life; social workers, teachers, even friends. I could not trust anyone. Mum was never violent towards me again and, somehow, the incident melted away, along with all the others. We had regular visits from social services but I kept my mouth zipped. I could not rely on them, or on anyone else. I was stuck in the cruellest of dilemmas. I wanted help. I wanted to escape the fear, but not my family. And yet my family was the fear. The very thing I wanted to run from was also the thing I cherished. My mother was my problem. But she was also my world.

6

CHRISTMAS 1996 came soon after. At school, there was great excitement as we rehearsed the Nativity, baked cute tree decorations out of dough and designed Christmas cards for our parents. For me, each activity only added to my growing despair. I had no chance of persuading my parents to buy me an angel costume to wear for the play. We had a Christmas tree at home, but it was a forlorn after-thought, usually hastily decorated by Dad on Christmas Eve and always involving a row with Mum. Neither of them would notice when I added my own hand-made decoration.

The other kids in class wrote lists for Santa and posted them into the letter box in the infant hall. Whilst they couldn't wait for Christmas Day, I dreaded it, not because I feared a lack of gifts, in fact quite the opposite. I hated to see my parents under extra pressure when they were already struggling. I saw Christmas not from a child's viewpoint but from a parent's. I worried constantly about who would pay for the gifts and, worse still, who would make the effort to buy them, wrap them and lay them out on Christmas Eve?

I felt nauseous just thinking about it. I would rather have had no gift at all than the avalanche of stress the festive season brought with it. Christmas morning dawned and Dad had, to his credit, ensured we all received one gift each. There were sweets and biscuits and cans of lemonade in the kitchen. But any festive cheer in the house was quickly wiped out the moment my parents were woken. Mornings were always fraught, and Christmas was no different. Dad lost his temper with Mum because she refused to get up and they argued, both on edge and in need of their daily bong.

"It's Christmas!" Dad yelled, as he kicked the mattress where Mum lay curled up with her face buried in a pillow.

"Yeah, I know!" she snapped. "So let me sleep."

I was in the kitchen when I heard him upending the mattress and I ran in to find Mum in a heap on the floor with her nose bleeding.

"Why do you have to hurt her?" I screamed. "Just leave her alone!"

Dad, uncharacteristically, did not shout back at me. Instead he slumped onto a chair and sank his head into his hands.

"I told your mother I didn't want all these children," he moaned. "I told her. This wasn't my idea."

His words were a punch in the stomach. Yet though they were unspeakably cruel, on Christmas of all days, my heart went out to him. He was lost, just as she was. Just as we all were.

"I'll get the little ones dressed and take them out for a bit," I offered. "Give you chance to have your bong."

If I was hoping for thanks, I was disappointed. Dad was already filing down a coconut shell to do the job, and he didn't even look up. But by the time we returned from the park it was almost lunchtime, and both my parents were stoned but friendly. It was the most I could hope for. My gift that year was a pink diary with a padlock and a small gold key. Dad knew I loved to write, and I was touched by his thoughtfulness. The key was soon lost amongst the mess at home and the padlock broke, but that didn't matter. I kept the diary under my pillow, though it was hardly a safe place for a secret. Yet where else? I felt untethered and unsettled in our house, with its lack of structure and routine. But at the same time, I was hemmed in and smothered.

There was a woeful lack of privacy; nothing was my own. I shared a bed, a bath, clothes, food; everything. And even though I was cramped up and squashed up most of the time, I felt painfully isolated and lonely. My identity was fuzzy and uncertain; who was I? How could I define myself when I did not even own my own toothbrush? And was this lack of privacy attached to a lack of worth? Was this why I was abused by Grampy? Was this the best that a child like me could hope for? The questions circled like flies, yet I was no nearer to solutions. That Christmas, Grampy bought selection boxes for all of my siblings. But when I visited him, the weekend before New Year, there were three large gifts waiting for me. My eyes grew wide as I unwrapped a Barbie doll, a Barbie horse, and a Barbie trailer.

"Wow, Grampy," I smiled. "Thank you."

"You're my girl," he said, resting his hand for just a moment on my leg.

I loved the presents, but even as I was tidying away the wrappings, a loud warning bell clanged at the back of my head. Why was I being singled out for extravagant gifts? Did this mean I was special? Or was the abuse a trade-off for a Barbie trailer? The thought choked me.

"Let's leave these new toys here at my house," Grampy suggested, as he snapped open a can of lager.

The knowledge that he was buying my silence with a heap of cheap plastic made my skin burn with shame. Yet at the same time, I was genuinely thrilled with my new Barbie. I'd never had my own doll before. Yet I felt guilty for my siblings and their measly selection boxes. They'd have loved a Barbie too. I didn't want them to know that I was different. I didn't even want to be different. But then, nobody ever asked me what I wanted. The conflict of emotions, the confusion and contradiction, was almost as bad as the abuse itself.

A few weeks after Christmas, into 1997, I went for my usual weekend at Grampy's. That Saturday night, he was nowhere to be seen at bathtime, which did not bring me the relief you might expect. Instead, I was on tenterhooks, my ears straining for the sharp sound of a ring pull or his throaty grunt on the stairs. Even as I climbed into the big double bed, I could not shake my feeling of unease. Just as I was falling asleep, I heard it. The unmistakable snap as he opened a can of lager. Each footstep on the staircase filled me with fright. Grampy smiled as he reached my door and settled himself on the edge of the ivory bedspread.

"I bought a new book about spirituality," he said, holding it up for me to see. "I think you'll like it. I'll read it to you now."

He claimed more and more to be interested in the spiritual world; a factor which had bonded me to him but was doubtless just another grooming technique, and the irony of him being in touch with his own spirituality sticks sharply in my throat. He held the first page open with one hand whilst the other clutched mine.

"This chapter is about connecting with your spirit guide," he told me.

It was not a book for children, but I listened obediently. And even then, during something as harmless as a bedtime story, his mere presence on my bed sent tremors through me. The fear leaked through my bones and made my teeth chatter. Suddenly, the big bed no longer felt quite so comfy or luxurious. I hated the gratuitous space and the swollen silence. I imagined the whispers from the ghosts in the walls as they braced themselves for what we all knew was coming. Partway through the chapter, Grampy abruptly put down his book. Every muscle in my body clenched in protest as his clammy hands slithered like snakes under the crisp white sheets.

"Please, Grampy," I whispered. "Please."

A stab of pain took my breath away. Again, I hurried to another place, a room so far back in the channels of my mind that I could escape this completely.

"Tomorrow is a new day," I told myself as I stumbled away. "This will not last."

Afterwards, I lay frozen in bed, pinned in place by my own trauma. This was the last place I wanted to be, I hated this boastful room, this fancy bed, this unnecessary space. Yet I could not leave it. Besides, I had nowhere else to go. I had a terrifying glimpse of my mother, cowering on her mattress, and in that moment, I felt her helplessness.

The following day, Grampy took me home, swinging the customary bag of Jaffa cakes over his arm. I was too big, mercifully, to go on his shoulders now, and instead he held my hand as we walked. Again, I struggled with the contradictions; these fingers had caused me untold pain and suffering. And yet, I liked holding Grampy's hand. I wanted to feel protected, guided and loved. Nobody else wanted to hold my hand; at home, it was the other way round.

The little ones clustered around Grampy when we arrived, thrilled by the sweet treats. Mum was happy to see him too. She sat up straighter on the sofa and her face brightened. More inconsistency. More confusion. Why was she so pleased to see him, after what he had done to us both? I ran to my bedroom, anxieties circling like crows around and around my head.

The sound of their friendly chatter floating up the stairs

seemed to scoff at what I had been through. Pulling my diary from under my pillow, I began to write: 'Why am I sent to Grampy's on my own?'

'Am I pregnant?'

'Why does Grampy bath me? Is it because I am good or bad?'

Seeing it written down in my childish scrawl was both comforting and shocking in equal measure. This was the first time I had shared my anguish, and even though I'd only told my diary, I felt my burden lift a little. The next day, I wrote more.

'Will Mum ever stop taking drugs? Will she die?'

'Will I go into care? Will I be separated from the little ones? Who will look after them?'

'Is it okay for a nine-year-old girl to watch rude films on telly?'

'Bad things at home or bad things at Grampy's? Why are these my only choices?'

I began confiding in my diary as though I would a friend. Each day, I wrote the date neatly at the top of the page, before my darkest fears spilled like black oil onto the white paper. There were so many questions and no replies. I wished, desperately, that someone would read my diary. I was not hopeful of any solutions, but I wanted, I needed, a sign that I was loved. One day, I had the brilliant idea of leaving my diary in the kitchen. Maybe if Mum found it, she would read it and understand how miserable I was. Filled with hope, I opened it to a page which said: 'I am scared and sad.'

I placed my diary next to a block of cannabis, knowing she couldn't fail to notice it, and then I went to bed. The following afternoon, when I got home from school, the cannabis had moved but my diary had not. Ignoring the twinge of disappointment, I decided to try again, this time leaving it on the living room sofa. For a few days, nothing happened. But one evening, Dad settled himself down to watch TV and picked up the diary. My mouth ran dry; I could hardly bear to watch. He flicked through a few pages, raised his eyebrows, and then laughed unkindly.

"Here," he said, handing the diary back to me. "Put this away."

He might just as well have spat in my face. This was worse even than it going unnoticed. Wilting like a dying flower, I traipsed upstairs. Of all the responses I'd envisaged, derision was not one. And if Dad found my diary amusing, surely this was more proof that Grampy's abuse was not wrong. Maybe I was the problem, and not Grampy? Racked with more self-doubt and self-loathing, in the end I had no choice but to confide again in my diary. There was some catharsis in that, though I knew now that help would never come. My 10th birthday brought with it more angst, as I worried about how and where my parents would find me a gift. I didn't even want a birthday present. It just wasn't worth the misery. Every day, I was on high alert as I waited for the next inevitable disaster, the next all-consuming crisis. Adding in the pressure of an unwanted birthday was enough to push our household into meltdown and I felt nothing but relief when it was finally over. A few days later, one of Dad's friends called round. He had children of his own and seemed nicer than our usual visitors.

"I heard it was your birthday, Tara," he smiled.

To my delight, he produced a £10 note.

"And make sure you buy something for yourself," he added. "The next time I'm here, I want to see what you chose."

I was thrilled. There were plenty of £10 notes, bundled up around our house. But this one was different, untainted by the toxicity of drugs. And the strict instruction to spend it solely on myself was so exciting. I had the perfect purchase in mind. That same afternoon, I walked all the way to Pets At Home in the town centre. Wandering up and down the aisles, I peered at the cages of white mice, hamsters and rabbits.

"What can I get for £10, please?" I asked the assistant.

"You can afford a hamster, along with a small cage and a bag of food," she calculated. "But really you should have an adult here with you when you buy."

I hesitated before slipping effortlessly into role-playing, as far away from my own reality as it was possible.

"Oh, my mum is in the car outside with my baby sister who's asleep," I explained. "She sent me in here to spend my birthday money. She's just outside, I promise you. Go and check if you like."

I was, through practice, a convincing liar and the assistant nodded and smiled. I was soon the proud owner of a small brown hamster who I named Hammy. Carrying everything home on my own was a struggle, but I'd never felt so happy. I settled his cage into a corner of the bedroom and then scooped him out onto my lap. I spent hours fussing over him, holding him up to my face, enjoying his furry feel against my skin.

"I love you, Hammy," I murmured, and I swear he squeaked it back.

Each day, after school, I lifted him out of his cage and carried him round the house in the front pocket of my skirt. At night, he slept on the pillow next to me. For the first time, I had good news to tell my diary.

'I have a best friend!' I announced. 'Hammy the Hamster!'

I was even allowed to take him to Grampy's in his cage, as long as I didn't let him run around the house. Hammy somehow made the abuse more bearable. Afterwards, he would stare at me intently with his bright eyes and I knew he was telling me: 'Don't worry, Tara, I'm here for you. Tomorrow will soon be here.'

I'd had Hammy maybe four or five months when I noticed a small swelling at the side of his head. At first, I thought it was just a bump, and I patted him better. But instead of subsiding, it got bigger.

"Look, Dad," I said, holding Hammy out for inspection. "What's wrong with him?"

"How should I know?" he shrugged, already disinterested.

I did everything I could to make Hammy well again. When Dad was snoozing, I helped myself to some loose change and bought carrots and apples from the local shop. But though they were his favourite treat, Hammy could not be tempted. As the lump grew, he lost his appetite and his sparkle. And I lost my own too. I couldn't bear to see him suffer.

"Please, Dad, can I take him to the vet?" I pleaded. "Please!"

But Dad wouldn't hear of it. Vets were money-grabbers, not to be trusted, and on the same banned list as police officers, social workers and teachers. I felt so helpless. I didn't even know where the nearest vet was, and I had no money to pay for treatment. I knew Dad would lose his temper if I defied him, but one Monday morning, I decided to do so regardless.

"After school, I'm going to find a vet and we'll see what they say," I told Hammy. "I'll find the money somehow. I promise. We'll soon have you better."

That afternoon, I rushed home and went straight upstairs. Hammy was sleeping, with his four small paws sticking straight up in the air. It was only as I reached out to touch him that I realised he was stiff and cold. He had been dead for some time. Cradling his lifeless body, I sobbed and sobbed, the tears splashing down onto his fur.

"I'm sorry," I wept. "I'm so sorry."

I refused to let go of him, believing I could somehow love

him back to life. But it was not to be. He was the only living being I loved who had loved me back. That night in my diary, I wrote: 'My heart is in pieces. I wish I was with Hammy.'

7

ONE SUNNY afternoon in the summer holidays, Dad announced we were going for a picnic.

"Get your shoes and coats on!" he grinned. "I've made jam sandwiches. I've got crisps and mini rolls!"

Tumbling over each other with excitement, we followed him up to the fields behind our estate. Dad seemed in a good mood as he handed out mini bottles of lemonade and bags of salt and vinegar crisps.

"Right," he said. "Who wants to see the sheep and the cows?"

There was a farm nearby and we had great fun mooing at the cows and screaming when they mooed back. My little sister, Jasmine, was still eating her bag of crisps and was chased across the yard by a gaggle of hungry geese, much to our amusement. Afterwards, we walked home and I was filled with the wholesome, healthy feeling which comes from being part of a normal family; a cog in a smoothly running wheel.

The other kids at school were off to caravan parks by the sea or Spanish hotels with swimming pools. But that one picnic in our summer holidays was a small burst of happiness and it meant everything to me. After that first day out, I began planning more. I decided we didn't have to mope around the house listening to my parents argue or hang around in the street outside waiting for them to calm down. I helped myself matter-of-factly to cash from Dad's jeans pocket and stocked up on my idea of picnic essentials; penny chews, fizzy pop and chocolate teacakes.

Jasmine was too scared of the geese to return to the farm. But we were happy to spread our coats in the field, stuff ourselves with as many sweets and chocolates as we could stomach and then make daisy chains or search for ladybirds amongst the long grasses. We built a base, a collection of leaves and twigs, and played manhunt. Other days, we practised songs and dance routines from our favourite bands; B*Witched and the Corrs.

'I would run away, I would run away, yeah, yeah…'

Ironically, though I spent my days dreaming of running away, I was perfectly content there, singing and dancing in the long grass. The fields offered tranquillity and temporary escape. It was always my job to pick up the discarded sweet wrappers, to kiss better the insect bites, to hold sticky little hands on the walk home. It was always my job to be Mum. But those days out were pocket-sized portions of happiness, and we treasured them.

In my last year at primary school, I was allowed to return

home at lunchtimes. This meant I not only avoided long, lonely playtimes on my own in the toilets, but I also didn't have to undergo the humiliation of being turned away in the dinner queue with my free meals form unsigned. And the real bonus was being able to check on Mum. I worried so much about her during the school day and just finding that she was still alive was enough to bring me to tears of relief. In that first week of term, I arrived home one lunchtime to find her busy making up wraps of amphetamine.

"Here, make yourself useful," she smiled, pushing a pile over to me.

I spent my entire lunchtime making wraps, and made such good progress that Mum said, "Don't go back to school, stay off and help me instead."

I didn't approve of her selling drugs, but I was pleased to have the afternoon off school. I was thrilled to be close to Mum, to share a chore and a hobby, even if it was drug related. I craved that connection.

Sometimes, I'd make wraps until late at night. I learned how to cut the amphetamine with glucose, before weighing it out and parcelling it up in small squares of newspaper. I was trusted to hand them out to the strangers who knocked on our door and sometimes even to deliver them around the estate. Aged 10, I could not see it for what it was, and I was just pleased that Mum was involving me.

By the end of the night there was always a huge pile of money on the table, and yet there was no food in our cupboards and no carpets on the floors. Even as a kid, I could see that something didn't quite add up. One evening, I was given instructions to take delivery of a nine bar - a 9oz block of cannabis resin. Mum was mid-way through one of her long sleeps and Dad was going out.

"Don't let him in," Dad ordered. "Take the nine bar and give him the cash at the door."

I hated dealing with the big suppliers, but I had no choice. When the delivery came, I was confronted by a large, bald, aggressive-looking man. His shoulders blocked the doorway as he stared wordlessly at me. When he stepped past me into the hallway, I was too intimidated to object. I put the block of cannabis he'd handed me down on a chair whilst I fumbled the notes together to make the payment. After he'd gone, I flopped onto the sofa with relief. At least it had gone well. When Dad arrived home later, he asked, "Where did you put the nine bar?"

As I pointed to the chair, my stomach lurched. There was nothing there.

"It must be here somewhere," I stuttered, looking under the chair. "It must be."

Dad's face grew purple as I crawled along the floorboards.

"You let him in didn't you, you silly little cow!" he bawled. "He's nicked it! Taken our money and our drugs! We've no money for food, thanks to you."

Incensed, he picked me up by my hair and dragged me through the house, shouting and swearing as he went. I sobbed, more from guilt than pain. I was responsible for the little ones starving. It was my fault they would not eat tomorrow. The glaring reality was that we never had money for food anyway. But that was no comfort to me either.

"I'm sorry," I sobbed, as I felt a clump of hair rip from my scalp. "I'm sorry."

That Christmas, I was, as always, racked with worry over the extra expense and pressure. During Christmas week, just after school had finished, a woman knocked on the door carrying a bin bag filled with wrapped gifts.

"These are for you," she smiled. "Happy Christmas!"

I mumbled an awkward thank you, but my insides were churning. It was mortifying to accept charity from a complete stranger. Besides, we had wads of cash stashed all over the house. We were not short of money – we were just short of someone to spend it on us. I felt both ashamed and fraudulent as I stacked her gifts under our balding Christmas tree.

I turned 11 in February 1998, and again my hope was, perversely, that I would receive nothing. It was easier for everyone that way. My visits to Grampy continued, with gifts of sweets and money alongside the abuse. His behaviour would have been more straightforward for me to process if he had been vile all the time. I would have preferred him to scream at me and beat me rather than confuse my mind with smiles and sick bribes. The inconsistency was, in itself, a form of abuse.

"My girl," he said proudly. "You're so special."

I had once loved to hear his compliments but now they turned my stomach. During each attack, I hurried off to hide in the far corners of my head. I could almost hear my own footsteps as I ran and feel the tightness in my chest as my breaths quickened. I was so desperate to escape. In the bathroom, I relied always on the birds to rescue me, and they never let me down.

'This will be over. You will survive. Tomorrow will soon be here.'

Hardest of all to reconcile, as an adult, is that there was much to enjoy during those weekends. When Grampy was not drinking, he was avuncular, funny and kind. He was generous both with his time and his money. He was the only relative I had who ever really listened to me. He asked about my school day in a way which suggested he was genuinely interested. He cooked for me; he bought my favourite treats. He had an old radio cassette player and bought me blank tapes so I could tape the Top 40 on Sunday evenings.

It was impossible to marry up these two versions of him, just as it was with my mother. More than anything, I wanted to believe that I was loved by this Jekyll and Hyde character. I clung to that. I made excuses for him, even during the abuse. Ever the budding psychologist, I wondered how and why he had turned out like this. He seemed almost reticent or regretful at times. Though that never stopped him. He was never violent; he did not use threats and instead showered me with what I believed were compliments.

"You're different, Tara. You're just like your mother."

And despite everything, I loved to hear the comparison. I relied on the monster who had hurt me to soothe my wounds. But the comment about my mother cleaved me in two. I longed so much to be like her. Yet I was terrified of being like her. After each thought, an opposing one followed. I did not know how to think. And being passed between two hellholes, between two equally destructive environments, traumatised me all the more.

* * * *

One weekend that February, Grampy settled back on the sofa, rolled up his sleeves, and pressed play on yet another disgusting film. I heard his customary little grunt as his breathing grew jagged, and my stomach turned in disgust. I had not planned to protest but it was as though my body was acting in isolation from my brain. I shocked myself as I stood up and said, "I'm not watching this."

There was a dangerous silence before Grampy replied, "Sit down."

Though he did not raise his voice, I was chilled by his tone. Yet I told myself I was not scared of him. I was determined for him not to crush me as he had crushed my mother. I had not told him I knew about his abuse of Mum. I did not know how to word it and if I did, I was frightened he might expect more of me. Mum's trauma became yet another corrosive secret that I was forced to keep. Every secret was a small crack but, as time passed, they had grown into one single bleeding wound. I was filled with shame, so deep I was drowning in it. But I was not about to let him know that.

"I'll sit down," I told him levelly. "But next time, I might not."

That small defiance was the first step, and I knew I would have to be brave to take the second. But I also knew I could not stand much more of this. I sat quietly, my heart beating too fast, my palms sweating. By the time the film finished, I felt like I had 1,000 mites burrowing into my skin. I felt dirty and contaminated. The moment I arrived home on Sunday evening, I ran myself a hot bath. Locking the door behind me, I scrubbed and scrubbed at my skin until it was red and raw. Yet still, I did not feel clean. My skin itched as though I was diseased. Which, I told myself, I probably was. Long after it was washed away, Grampy's pungent stench lingered on in my mind and somehow leaked out through my skin. I smelled it constantly. I got into the habit of bathing four, even five, times a day, desperate to rid myself of a poison which I knew was on the inside. And baths were, of course, part of the problem; as much about trauma as solace. I could not run the water without imagining Grampy's hands creeping up my legs like spiders. A hot bath was liquid terror. And yet still, I washed and scrubbed, emptying all the lotions we had, whilst knowing nothing would ever make any difference.

Somehow, I struggled on through that final year of primary school, juggling the same toxic set of circumstances; physical and mental abuse from my parents, sexual abuse from my grandfather, worry and stress over the welfare of my younger siblings. There was no space or time to think about myself. Early one evening, in the summer holidays, I hid in my room and clamped my hands over my ears as my parents fought over a missing bag of amphetamine. I missed Hammy so much at times like this. I heard a smash and realised another window had been sacrificed. Wearily, I accepted it would be my job to sweep the broken glass and, though I had done it many times before, the task suddenly felt impossible. At 11, I was so tired of life. Each day brought different problems but the same weary sense of despair. I was stuck on a grim carousel, going round and round with no end in sight.

'I cannot take any more of it,' I wrote in my diary. 'I don't want to live like this.'

I found a carrier bag and packed my diary, a warm jumper, and my favourite blue Care Bear. I was ready. But I could not go without first putting the little ones to bed; if not me, then who? When they were safely tucked in, I kissed them in turn and picked up my bag.

"I love you all," I said softly.

Once outside, I was unsure of my next step. I had planned to run away without really knowing where I would go. It was still light, and so I made my way to the same field where I'd often taken the little ones for picnics. It wasn't so much fun on my own and, as the light faded, it grew spooky too. Perhaps, I told myself, someone would miss me, now it was dark. Maybe my parents would even come out to look for me. I was, after all, a missing child. It got late and I started to worry about where I might sleep, what I would eat, and, worst of all, who would look after the little ones now I was gone? Who would run to the shop for milk, find a missing sock, rub a grazed elbow? I could not walk out on them all.

Clutching my Care Bear, I decided I had made my point. My parents would surely be frantic by now. I half-expected to see a search party combing the estate. But our street, as I turned the corner, was deserted. The tell-tale smell of cannabis drifting from the windows of my home was proof that someone was still awake. I crept to the living room window and peered inside.

My parents were slumped on the sofa, their feet up on the mattress, watching TV without a care in the world. I let myself in the back door and went upstairs, with the mortifying realisation that nobody had even noticed I was gone.

8

THAT SEPTEMBER, I was due to start at high school. We'd had a letter offering financial help with uniforms, but nobody filled in the accompanying forms and so the money never came. That first day, I had no choice but to turn up at school in a pair of black combat trousers and a dark coloured jumper with a white t-shirt underneath. It was the closest I could get to a school uniform. I convinced myself that I might somehow go under the radar, but instead, as I queued for the welcome assembly, a teacher pulled me aside.

"Here," she said, handing me a discoloured shirt and tie. "Go and put these on quickly."

It was mortifying to hear the sniggers of the other kids in the line as she spoke. Like any child, my one wish starting high school was to blend in seamlessly. Now, I was marked out, not only as different, but as an object of disgust or pity. A charity case. Pulling the shirt over my head in the toilets, I caught a whiff of stale sweat and smoke and felt a sad affinity with the other kids who had worn this before me. But as the days passed, I grew a tougher shell. I had no option.

"Why are you wearing combat trousers?" barked the deputy head one morning.

"Because I don't like my school trousers," I quipped. "They're horrible."

It was a lie. But at least this way, I was saving face and taking back a little bit of control. I was sent to see a support teacher who gave me a second-hand uniform. Even so, I felt like an outcast. My family background, my badly fitting uniform, my crippling lack of self-confidence, all made me easy prey for the bullies. I wanted to like school, more than anything I wanted to fit in, but my thoughts were usually elsewhere. In maths, which I hated, I'd make mental lists of my chores for the day; there was a pile of dirty laundry in the kitchen, and we had no food in for dinner. I enjoyed history and, surprisingly, RE. Though I wasn't at all religious, I grasped at the idea of prayer as a way of changing my situation. Each night, I offered a silent plea for intervention – divine or otherwise. I was in my first term at high school when, one afternoon, we had a talk from a youth worker, warning about the dangers of drugs. There were a couple of jokes at my expense as his slideshow played on the overhead projector.

"Tara, you could give us a talk on drugs, couldn't you? Bring in some samples!"

The rest of the class giggled whilst my cheeks burned. I wanted to sink right through the floor. I distracted myself by worrying about my little sister, who had refused her breakfast and hadn't seemed well that morning. But when the youth worker mentioned amphetamines, my mother's drug of choice, I suddenly snapped to attention.

"Long term amphetamine abuse can lead to weight loss, dental problems, paranoia and hallucinations," he said. "It can even cause heart attacks, strokes and death. Amphetamines are especially harmful to unborn babies during pregnancy."

My own heart stuttered. For years I had worried Mum might die from drugs and I was right to do so. She had recently announced she was pregnant again and so was risking the baby's life as well as her own. As soon as the talk was over, I spoke to the youth worker and asked for the printout on amphetamines. In spite of my world-weariness, I was still naïve enough to believe a printed sheet and some good advice might be all Mum needed to kick the drugs.

"Here," I said, thrusting it into her hand that evening.

When she refused to read the printout herself, I read it out loud, sitting on the edge of her mattress as I highlighted the salient points.

"What do you think?" I asked. "Could you give it a try, Mum, please? Maybe cut down a bit? This stuff could kill you."

But she did not even reply. I had been an idiot to believe things would ever change and irrationally, I blamed myself. How could I have been so foolish? Drugs were more important to my parents than life itself. And soon after, their loyalty was tested in the cruellest way imaginable. After starting high school, I'd noticed a few spots on my forehead and chin and inevitably, the bullies noticed them too. I was desperate not to give them more ammunition and so the next time Mum announced a late-night sweep of the supermarket shelves, I asked if I could go along with her.

"I need spot cream," I explained. "Would you be able to get it for me?"

"Yeah okay," she grinned. "Why not?"

The little ones were all in bed except Jasmine, who was three years old and playing happily with a toy on the sofa. Leaving Dad in charge, Mum and I went off to Asda where she stole a tube of spot cream; possibly one of the only promises she had ever kept. I was so pleased with the cream, partly because I needed it but more so because it was a gift from my mother and I saw it as a sign of her love. When we arrived back home, I noticed Jasmine was hunched up on the sofa with her head lolling. I thought she'd fallen asleep.

"Jazzy!" I said softly. "Time for bed!"

But when I took her face in my hand, I gasped. Her eyes were wide open, staring right through me, and her skin was clammy.

"What's wrong with her?" I asked. "Look! She's ill."

Dad turned his head slowly.

"She swallowed something," he admitted. "A lump of weed. Not a lot. She'll be fine."

I glared at him in disbelief. This was jaw-dropping, even from him.

"She's not fine," I said, my voice wobbling. "She needs a doctor."

I turned to Mum for support, but she was busy building herself a bong. She didn't seem to hear me.

"Jazzy, Jazzy," I spluttered, but she didn't respond.

Panic rose within me like a tidal wave, filling my chest with a cold white dread. I had thought I was well acquainted with fear; the late-night raiders who smashed up our home, the attacks by Grampy, Dad's rages. But this was true terror. I felt myself disintegrating in horror, my legs giving way under me.

"Please, can we take her to hospital," I pleaded. "Let's get her checked out. Please!"

Dad slammed his can down onto the arm of the sofa so violently it fizzed up and spilled all over his hand.

"Let's be clear," he snarled. "If you take your little sister to hospital, or if you even breathe a word of this to anyone, we are in big shit. Your Mum and me will go to prison and you kids will all go into care. Is that what you want, eh, little Miss Angelica? Sticking your nose in again where you're not wanted?"

Yet again, I was pulled between two impossible and imperfect choices. I might as well have been pulled in two myself; the agony was physical. I knew Dad was probably right. If social services found out Jasmine had swallowed drugs, they'd take us all away. Besides, my parents would doubtless deny everything. Maybe they would even blame me, and I would go to prison in their place. These were all risks I could not take. And yet if we did nothing, my little sister might not survive.

"What if she dies?" I asked, tears streaking down my cheeks.

Dad snorted scornfully.

"Course she won't die," he scoffed. "She just needs to sleep it off. It's her own silly fault, going round putting everything in her mouth. This will teach her."

I didn't know what to do. My parents clearly were not going to help. As always, I was on my own with this. Jasmine was floppy and woozy as I carried her upstairs to the bedroom. I tried to give her a drink of water but most of it dribbled back out again. Settling her on the bottom bunk next to another sister, I got a blanket and pillow so I could sleep on the floor beside her. The hours dragged agonisingly slowly as I stayed awake, holding her hand. Every time she drifted off to sleep, I worried she was dying, and I roused her again with a flick on her cheek. Her skin was pale, with a sweaty sheen like clingfilm across her face.

"Please don't die, Jazzy," I begged. "Please don't leave me."

I became so worried, I resolved to dial 999 and deal with Dad's fury later. But then I remembered our house phone had been disconnected, and I'd have to leave the house to use the phone box on the corner. I could not risk leaving Jasmine on her own. It was the cruellest dilemma; stay with my sister and watch her die or run for help and risk her dying alone. It felt like the longest night and to comfort myself, I repeated my well-worn mantra, chanting it like a prayer under my breath. It seemed more poignant now than ever:

'This won't last. Everything passes. Tomorrow will come. Tomorrow will come, Jazzy.'

Gazing at her little button nose and her pursed up mouth, I telegraphed reassurance and love, stability and safety, in a house where there was none. Eventually, the first pink streaks of light outside brought some small relief. Jasmine lay motionless and quiet in the bunk. I hadn't slept at all; I was dizzy with exhaustion, terrified she might still be in danger and angry my parents had dismissed her so glibly. There was a knock at the front door and too late I remembered I'd arranged to meet Cassie, a girl from my estate, so we could walk to school together. I'd promised to be at the top of the street for 8.30am. She was my only real friend, and I knew I had to keep her away from our house if I wanted our friendship to last. She knocked again and I went downstairs, opening the door just a crack and peering round it.

"Morning Tara, when you weren't there I thought you might have overslept," she smiled.

"No," I sniffed. "Nothing like that. I'm just not feeling very well. I'm not going in today."

"Let me come in," she said, her face creased with concern. "What's the matter? I want to help you."

But I had closed the door before she could even finish her sentence. I was so ashamed of my home, of my family, of myself. I could not bear for her to see it. I hurried back upstairs to Jasmine, who slowly improved as the day went on. Though she was quiet and a little hazy, I managed to get her to eat cereal at lunchtime. And by around 6pm, she was almost back to her usual self. Dad smirked as Jasmine toddled past him in the kitchen.

"See," he told me. "I was right all along. You need to stop interfering in other people's business. I'm the parent here, not you."

If I hoped either of them might learn a lesson from it, then I was wrong. I begged Mum again to stop taking drugs, but she didn't even have the energy to lie to me. She shook her head sadly. She had no fight left. At school the next day, I did my best to convince Cassie I'd had a nasty stomach bug.

"I'm fine now," I insisted. "But it's best if I meet you on the street corner in future. My house is chaotic, so many kids!"

"I don't mind that," she smiled.

But again, the actress in me was desperate to keep the truth hidden for as long as I could. It was no secret that my parents were drug dealers; most of the neighbourhood knew that. But it was the neglect and abuse which shamed me the most. I didn't want Cassie to call round and see my mother prone on a mattress in the living room, witness the empty cupboards, the disconnected utilities, the guilty piles of cash. I could not let her see the real me. I was convinced the smell of drugs oozed from my skin, which was all the more reason to bath several times a day; I was scrubbing at the smell of cannabis as well as the stench of abuse. I made sure to wash my uniform each night after school too. I had only one of each item and sometimes went to school wearing damp clothes, but it was better than stinking of drugs.

"Tara, you've nothing to be embarrassed about," Cassie insisted again.

But, as with the abuse, I kept my friends at a distance. I did not, could not, allow myself to open up. Life continued at a steady level of despair punctuated by moments of great trauma. And soon, the drama of Jasmine's overdose was usurped by something else. The trouble began with a police raid on our home which was not especially unusual. The house was in semi-darkness because our electricity had been disconnected, which made the strangers marauding through our home even more alarming. My parents were kept downstairs. I was ushered into my bedroom with an officer right behind me.

"Where are the drugs?" he demanded. "Tell me, and this can all stop."

Truthfully, I had no idea, but I would not have told him even I did. I knew better than that. I watched silently as he and another officer pulled our belongings out of drawers and the wardrobe. I cringed as they upended a cardboard box serving as a laundry basket and containing all our dirty underwear. Our clothes were not washed regularly, and I was humiliated to see our slovenly habits exposed and our privacy violated, as though we did not matter.

"Take your top off," barked one of the officers.

He was around 30 years old with a mean face. I imagined he didn't smile much.

"What?" I spluttered. "No, I won't."

He reached forward and yanked my t-shirt over my head. I was wearing a training bra and my first thought, bizarrely, was that he would be dissatisfied. I was not yet fully developed, and I worried he'd be annoyed; somehow cheated and short-changed. What if, because I wasn't enough, he targeted one of my younger sisters instead? The suggestion left me paralysed with panic. I stared at the floor whilst he reached round and unclasped my bra. His hands were cold on my warm skin and, as he dropped my bra, he grabbed at one breast and squeezed hard. It was over in a flash; I could almost kid myself I had imagined it, or I had misunderstood. I could tell myself it hadn't happened. Yet it had.

"Put that back on!" he said, nodding at my t-shirt.

At the door as he left, he shouted, "All clear!"

My primary feeling, as I got dressed, was one of relief. He had spared my little sisters and so I must have been adequate, after all. Out on the landing, it was chaos; our belongings scattered like litter, heavy boots clattering down the stairs as the officers left. Robotically, I began tidying up, comforting the little ones who had lost a favourite teddy, a soother, a drink of juice, in all the mess. My parents were furious, ranting and swearing against the system. It was not until later, when my siblings were in bed, that I was hit by the full enormity of what had happened.

Reliving the assault was like being hit with a breeze block. This was confirmation, if ever I needed any, that I was worthless, pointless, useless. I mattered so little that a serving on duty police officer had no qualms about sexually assaulting me in my own home.

As a child of drug dealers, I was fair game, easy pickings. Perhaps it was tattooed across my forehead. Grampy saw it. And now this policeman had seen it too. Maybe, as I had feared, abuse did have its own particular stench. Perhaps there was a smell which percolated from my every pore, alerting other predators and attracting them to me. They picked up the scent like wolves hunting prey.

My despair gathered pace, like a snowball, until it grew into a full-blown avalanche, burying me under a ton of snow. I checked that Mum was settled on her mattress and then I went out. Even then, as I slipped on my denim jacket, I felt his cold fingers on my skin. They were still there. And I knew, no matter how much I showered or bathed, they would be there always. I'd helped myself to a £10 note from Dad's coat and went straight to the corner shop, where the owner helpfully turned a blind eye to under-age drinkers.

I bought a bottle of Mad Dog 20/20 because it was the cheapest and quickest way of getting drunk. Finding a bench nearby, I gulped down mouthfuls, hoping to blot out the pain. Instead, like unwanted guests, snippets of memory forced their way in… Grampy forcing my head down, his sleeves rolled up, his watch glinting as it caught the light. Mum sobbing like a child in my arms, her hair plastered to her face. Dad's mouth wide open, spittle flying, as he yelled at me. The leering police officer, his hand clamped onto my breast.

"This will pass," I told myself uncertainly, tipping the bottle back. "Tomorrow will come."

The thing was, I didn't want a tomorrow. Not anymore. I didn't want to feel like this ever again. I took another swig of 20/20, retching as I forced it down. Yet I felt remarkably clear-headed as I stood up, walked back to the corner shop, and used my spare change to buy a packet of paracetamol. I swallowed the lot and then went home. If it was not a conscious decision to die, it was certainly a definite vote against living. But before I even got into bed, my stomach began to heave. I spent most of the night hunched over the toilet, vomiting. I had never been so ill and yet I welcomed this physical pain, because it was at least a distraction from the agony in my head. In the early hours, Dad appeared at the bathroom door.

"Another hangover," he scoffed. "You're useless, you know that? Just like your mother. For all your interfering and your bossiness, you're a waste of space."

As my throat contracted again, I nodded weakly. He was absolutely right. I made a mess of everything. I couldn't even kill myself properly. By first light, my stomach was bruised but empty. And though I felt utterly miserable, there was still a glimmer of hope for a new day and a relief that I was here to see it. Despite everything, I was glad my overdose had failed.

"Everything passes," I reminded myself.

Reaching the lowest point, I had an instinct, like an inbuilt safety mechanism, to pull back and take stock. No matter what happened, I would not let this crush me. Much as I loved my parents, I was resolved not to end up like them. Even aged 12, I understood that people were not born as drug addicts or alcoholics. Unbearable pain and pressure had left my parents broken. As part of that chain, the expectation was that I would break also.

"No," I said out loud. "My link will stay strong. I won't be beaten."

But the next catastrophe to hit the family tested my resolve to the limit. Late one night, the little ones were in bed when Grampy let himself in through the back door, waving a video tape in his hand. I felt suddenly nauseous. Surely, he was not about to show my parents one of his explicit films.

"Did you see *Crimewatch* earlier?" he asked grimly. "You're famous."

His tone was even, but there was a hint of menace. He would never directly confront my father, much as he liked to criticise him privately.

"No, we didn't," Dad said. "What are you talking about?"

Grampy pushed the cassette into our video player and the

latest edition of BBC's *Crimewatch* began to play. Grampy fast-forwarded over the major crimes and reconstruction scenes, until he reached the part of the programme where officers made appeals in connection with smaller crimes.

'And in Swindon,' said the presenter. 'A police raid was carried out with a quantity of drugs and cash seized. Police are appealing for witnesses to identify the adults seen fleeing this scene.'

To my horror, grainy footage of our house appeared on the screen, as officers banged down the door and charged into the hallway. All hell let loose; there was shouting and swearing, strangers falling over themselves and each other to get out, my mother rooted to the spot, wailing and crying. And there in the background, for just a split second, was a frightened child in a Minnie Mouse nightdress, standing at the top of the stairs. Me. I was appalled. My first thought was the nightie was far too small for me and everyone at school would see my skinny legs and make fun of me. This was the last thing I needed when I was trying to make friends and blend in. And then, the wider implications hit me. The whole world could see the depths of our depravity; Mum howling like a banshee, Dad making himself scarce, various unknown addicts draped around our living room like forgotten items of clothing. The place was a drug den, not a family home, and our shame was laid bare, on the BBC for everyone to gawp at.

"You keep your mouths shut," Dad warned, as the footage ended.

And then he waggled his finger in my face: "Especially you, Miss Bossy Boots! If anyone asks you for names, you say nothing."

I was disgusted, but not surprised, that his only concern was him or his friends being reported to the police. As I lay awake in bed that night, I realised I was not even sure which raid was captured on that film. There had been so many attacks on our home, from police, from dealers, from disgruntled customers, that they all merged into one. I stretched my nightie down further over my knees. Even in bed, I felt uncomfortable, as though I was still being filmed. I was so unsafe, even at home. Especially at home. My status as an outcast was cemented after *Crimewatch* aired. Although our family hadn't been identified, and I had been nothing more than a blurry outline in a nightie, everyone at school knew it was me. I was an object of disgust for some and fascination for others, almost like I was another species entirely. Cassie, thankfully, was sympathetic.

"Take no notice of them all," she advised. "They'll find someone else to talk about soon. Anyway, it's none of their business."

Social services paid us another visit, and for a mad moment, I thought of breaking rank and screaming at the top of my lungs.

'My little sister swallowed drugs and nobody took her to hospital. Dad hits me and calls me names. Mum sleeps all day and keeps me off school to sell drugs. And Grampy…. Grampy….'

I could not articulate that, even to myself. It was too deeply interred. As I opened my mouth, my courage vanished. The fight was leaving me, just as it had left Mum. I flopped back onto the sofa and tuned out as the social worker issued a strict list of instructions and my parents made promises we all knew they would never keep. And whilst I wanted, needed, support, I was also mistrustful of it. What if I went into care, and never saw Mum or my siblings again? And who would look after them, after I was gone? Speaking to social services might be the best move or the biggest mistake I ever made. I could not take that gamble. Yet how could this situation be my only choice, trapped between two houses, each offering its own peculiar brand of torture.

9

WITH THE rush of hormones which arrived after my 13th birthday, my moods changed and, in particular, my attitude towards school. Previously, I had been generally quiet, well-behaved and solitary, anxious not to draw attention to myself. But now a defiance crept in, a mini uprising, aimed at all the adults I judged to have failed me – with the exception of my mother. I adored her, despite, or maybe because, of her flaws.

One afternoon in food technology, we were given a list of ingredients to buy, to bake a Victoria Sponge the following lesson. It was pointless asking my parents for money, never mind requesting they provide the ingredients. I could have stolen the cash, as I had many times before, but something inside me railed against that. Why should I? Why was this my problem? I was frustrated and resentful at the complete absence of support and understanding from all those in authority. But when I turned up the next week empty-handed, the teacher decided to make an example of me.

"You can spend the next hour writing out: 'I must not forget my cooking ingredients'," she told me.

Normally, I would have nodded my head obediently. But I was already feeling the stress of being in a food tech lesson, bringing back those memories of cooking with Grampy when I was small. As she spoke, I was plagued by savage flashbacks to the attacks in the bathroom and the spare room.

"It's not fair!" I shouted suddenly. "It's not my fault my parents won't buy me the stuff! Why can't I just borrow it?"

I pointed to the walk-in pantry behind her, where packets of sugar, flour and eggs sneered back at me.

"Oh no," she snapped, stepping into the pantry. "I know your type, Tara. You think you can waltz in here and expect everything done for you. Well that's not going to happen."

In that moment, I hated her. With a stab of anger, I slammed the pantry door shut in her face and grabbed my bag.

"I've had enough!" I yelled, hurling words behind me as I marched out of the classroom and out of the school.

"Enough!"

I was still flushed when I arrived home. Mum didn't ask why I was home early, or what was wrong, and simply nodded at a big bag of amphetamine.

"Give us a hand with this," she said, giggling as she made space for me on the sofa.

She was like a little girl, younger in many ways than I was, even though she was 34. Her voice was high-pitched and soft. She was, at heart, still the same small child she had been during her father's abuse. The trauma had somehow stunted her emotional development and left her so vulnerable and delicate that she might shatter under the slightest pressure. Her role as a local drug dealer was at odds with the innocence I saw in her. But I knew her best.

"I love having you home with me," Mum beamed.

And I felt just the same. I was suspended from school for the rest of the week and found it quite suited me. I needed to keep an eye on everyone at home. Ever since the school drugs talk, I had become paranoid Mum might die in her sleep. I liked being around so I could collect the little ones from primary school.

Even when my suspension was up, I was loathe to go back. What was the point? Who could make me? Rebellion rose like a hissing snake inside me. I went in for a couple of days but then I got into a row over a jibe someone had made about my little sister. I didn't care what people said about me, but I could not bear for my siblings to be bullied. I got myself into more and more trouble so that more often than not I was suspended. Eventually, I decided school was not for me. I was too old for it and in a way, I always had been.

"Not going back," I announced to Cassie. "I don't care what they say."

Yet behind the façade, I was still the same anxious little girl as before. Some days, I didn't go to school as a matter of principle. But other times I was busy looking after Mum or the littles ones. We never once went to the dentist, but I was responsible for organising doctors' appointments. We were not registered with a local surgery and so whenever anyone was ill, I had to call a walk-in centre. One of my little sisters had ongoing digestive issues and seemed to pick up one sickness bug after another. I often found myself at the walk-in centre, pushing a baby in a buggy and trailing another toddler behind me.

"We can't see her without an adult. Where are your parents?" asked the nurse.

Again, I stepped into my role as an Oscar-worthy actress.

"My dad works away in London and Mum's doing a late shift," I told them. "We've got a babysitter but she's at home with my other sister."

"Okay," she conceded, looking with concern at my sister. "Come on in."

Spinning this narrative, half-living a fairytale existence, I almost believed my own lies. They seemed to work too, and I congratulated myself that I had everyone fooled. Much later, I'd realise the nurse probably saw right through me and felt sorry for us. It was the same with parents' evenings. Mum turned up to the occasional one, but when I reached high school, they mostly became my responsibility.

"My Dad is working abroad, and Mum has a broken leg and can't leave the house," I told the teacher. "So they've sent me along instead."

The lies tripped so easily off my tongue. Besides, I wanted to be there for my siblings; their health and education were important to me. Like a miniature mother hen, I fluffed up with pride at their achievements and squawked angrily at disappointments. When I wasn't needed at home, I hung around the street corners or went to the park. There was a middle-aged woman, Sammy, living nearby who had a dubious open-house policy, and her home was filled with people smoking drugs, drinking and having sex. There is, I imagine, a house like this on every estate in every town. My friends and I started going round there, more out of boredom than anything else. But soon, I was drinking and smoking cannabis just like the rest of them.

I had grown up with such a strong antipathy towards drugs and I was, in some part, annoyed at myself. Worse still, I smoked not out of defiance, but defeat. I was engulfed by despair, happy to try anything which blocked out a bubbling cauldron of anxieties, if only temporarily. At weekends, the abuse from Grampy continued. I had always known it was wrong. And at high school, with sex education classes and lectures on personal boundaries and consent, I slowly realised that it was worse even than I had feared. Other grandfathers did not abuse their grandchildren. Other parents did not allow it to happen. It was not only immoral, but illegal too. Yet still, I scratched around in my mind for any excuse, any reason, to somehow explain or justify at least a part of his behaviour.

Could there be an explanation I had over-looked? The amateur psychologist in me was always looking for reasons and triggers. One evening, whilst me and Cassie were walking to the shop, I asked hesitantly, "Do your parents watch porn films at home?"

"What!" shrieked Cassie. "No, of course not. That would be weird. Do yours?"

"No," I stuttered. "No. I just wondered. That's all."

With no other outlet, I poured my anxieties out onto my diary pages: 'Why do my parents send me to Grampy's? Do they know he abuses me? Even if they don't, they know he abused Mum. So why take the chance?

'Does Grampy hate me? Why does he do it? Could he be ill? Maybe he doesn't know it's wrong?'

The page glared, mocking me silently.

'Of course he knows it's wrong, Tara. They all know it's wrong. Bad people do bad stuff. Just accept it.'

And yet still, I could not bear the reality of what he had done to me. And worse, to Mum. As an adult, I wonder why I was not angry with my mother. She had, after all, thrown me into the same lions' den where she herself had been mauled and devoured whole. What kind of mother would do that? The fact that she was a victim made her behaviour more unforgiveable. And yet, that's not how it was. As the facts congealed and my understanding solidified, I felt only sympathy for her. When she cried out during the night and I ran to her, she would confide further in me.

"Grampy made me have sex with him before I was allowed out to play," she sobbed. "And so I did it. I hate myself for it."

I held her close as she rocked back and forth in despair.

"I'm a terrible mother," she wept. "I've let you all down. I don't know what to do."

"Mum," I whispered, choking back my own tears. "You must never blame yourself. None of this was your fault."

In my mother's case, I was able to see the facts rationally and reasonably. Yet for myself, I did not detach quite so easily. I did not blame Mum for her own abuse or for mine. Yet I did blame myself. Each time Grampy attacked me, I held myself responsible. I couldn't help it. I was the one who was supposed to fix this family, and yet I was falling apart myself. How could it not be my fault?

* * * *

One weekend, towards the end of 2000, Grampy cracked open a can of super strength lager and flicked on the TV, ready for another disgusting film. I never got used to them, no matter how many I was forced to watch. I prepared myself to pull back, to disappear into another compartment in my head. These withdrawals took the form of a cold paralysis; they were like a nightmare, where I could follow events but not change them. But as the naked figures writhed on the screen, I had a sudden and savage moment of realisation, like a burst of bright light behind my eyes. I was ready, at last, for my second step.

"No," I said firmly. "I'm not watching this and you can't make me."

I expected a sharp rebuke, but Grampy must have sensed my resolve because instead, he looked at me curiously.

"And don't touch me again," I snapped, and I turned on my heel and walked out of the house.

I wish I could say I felt a rush of triumph or even relief. But I was instead swamped with shame. Crippled by it. Saying it out loud had made it real. There was no way round it. Grampy was an abuser. And I was his victim. As I walked down the street, I was sluiced through with sorrow. Why was my life like this? Was it my fault? Why was I punished, every living moment, just for being me?

The day was grey and dull as though someone had thrown a dark tarpaulin over the whole town. My steps slowed as it began to drizzle. Where exactly was I walking to? I couldn't go home; I couldn't face further stress and chaos. I didn't want to turn up at Sammy's on my own because I didn't feel safe. Perhaps I'd known all along that my only option was to return to Grampy's, to the lair of the enemy I had just escaped.

Even as I turned around, I felt tentacles from the house brushing my skin, tightening around my wrists and ankles. I said nothing to Grampy and instead went straight upstairs to listen to music on the cassette player. But lying on my bed, I knew something in the house had changed. I felt it in the air, a type of residual charge, almost like the lingering smell of gunpowder on November 6. I'd detonated an explosion and now there was no going back. Grampy must have felt it too. He did not challenge me when, that night, I locked the bathroom and bedroom doors to keep him out. In the months which followed, he continued to watch pornography, but I stayed out of the room. On occasions, he would get drunk and make a grab at me as I walked past him.

"Leave me alone," I told him fiercely.

Other times, he'd look me up and down approvingly.

"You're so like her," he said, a little breathless. "Really, you're so special."

"Yes, and I'm stronger than her," I hissed. "So keep your distance."

We did not need to name her. My mother was the victim at the epicentre of this, with rings of red-hot trauma around her. Much as I wanted to distance myself and carve a different path, I longed also to be like her. I treasured all comparisons with my mother, scooped them up like a hungry bird with stale breadcrumbs. Yet I held my nerve with my grandfather, and he never dared abuse me again. It is confusing, even for me, that I carried on visiting him. But I was a child and he was still my Grampy. And any love is better than none at all.

One evening, I was rummaging through Mum's latest haul from the skips, silently turning up my nose at the assortment of clothes and trinkets she'd found. Like most 14-year-olds, I had a clear idea of the image I wanted to portray. I liked denim jackets, gypsy tops, and hipster jeans with wide belts. But unfortunately, the skips didn't deliver to order. More than clothes, I loved toiletries and perfumes. My teenage spots were, if anything, getting worse, and I was forever researching the latest creams and lotions which might help. As I was getting to the bottom of the black bin bag, I pulled out a bottle of Chanel, almost full.

"Can I have this?" I said excitedly. "Can I?"

I sprayed my arm and breathed in the scent. It was beautiful; so classy and sophisticated. Mum delved back into the bin bag and held up a pink miniskirt, so short it might as well have been a belt.

"What about this, Tar?" she grinned, her face so animated it looked like she had been lit up.

I was about to say no but found myself nodding. Why not? I was often out in the evenings, either hanging round the shops or at Sammy's. I might as well dress up. I picked out a couple more items, a fitted top and some bracelets, to complete my outfit. And the tight mini skirt was, I soon found out, a sure-fire way to attract attention. Round at Sammy's, there were catcalls and murmurs of approval when I tottered in wearing a pair of Mum's stiletto boots.

"Legs 11!" someone shouted.

The fact that I was 14 years old didn't seem to bother anyone. I wish I could say I called them out for the predators and paedophiles they were. I wish I'd marched right back out again. But instead, I blushed with shy pleasure. Scratch under the smiling veneer, and I was a damaged child. Behind the bravado, I was mangled and crushed. Having escaped the clutches of my grandfather, I ought to have run a mile from men like this. Instead, I was pulled towards them, drawn to them like a magnet, for they were all I knew. I longed for these men to notice me, to compliment me, to validate my existence. I told myself attention was a form of affection. I reframed abuse as love. And so, as one form of abuse stopped, another tragically began.

My period came around that time. I knew from friends that this was supposed to be a special time, a marker for the end of childhood. But I could not confide in my mother and instead it became just another secret. I found a box of tampons in the bathroom but as I tore off the wrapper, I felt suddenly nauseous. In an instant I was back in Grampy's bathroom, slammed by flashbacks of his hands on my legs, that horrible grunting sound he made. I felt again the stinging pain of the assault, and I shoved the tampon back in the box. There was no way I could use a tampon; not then and never since. My phobia has followed me, like a cloud, right through my adult life. The memory is as raw today as it was in my teens. Instead, I resorted to emptying Dad's pockets of change and buying a pack of sanitary pads. There was no celebration, or even relief, at this solitary milestone. I was on the cusp of becoming a young woman and yet, in my mind, I had been old beyond my time for many years.

Dipping in and out of school as though it was optional, I split my time between looking after Mum and the littles ones and going out with a couple of the girls from our estate. I transformed, almost overnight, from a child in joggers and hoodies to a moody and inappropriately dressed teenager. I'd never worn make-up before and Mum didn't use it either, but she was happy enough to bring some back from her next Asda trip. My mates taught me how to knot my bra straps behind my neck to create a better cleavage, and how to draw a flick with my new eye-pencil.

Despite the superficial giggles and the shiny lipstick, I felt like an empty pinata; beaten so many times that I had burst and emptied out. I was hollow inside. The similarities with my mother were closer than I realised. Dressed up in our sky-high heels and skimpy outfits, me and my friends strutted along the bypass into town, counting the beeps of approval from the cars which drove past. Each beep was confirmation someone liked me. As a metaphor for all which was toxic in my life, I grew to rely on those car horns as a measure of my self-worth. One evening, I was hanging around the town centre with a couple of new mates, when two men approached us. One was tall, in his late 30s, maybe even early 40s. His friend was chubby and looked mid-30s.

"How do you girls fancy coming back to our place?" they asked.

"How do we know you're not serial killers?" I quipped.

"Well, I'm a copper, so you can trust me," the taller one replied, flashing me a smile.

I had no idea if he was a police officer and I had no way of finding out. I didn't trust anyone, especially the police, but we piled into his car regardless and he took us to a house in Swindon.

"What do you want to drink?" he asked.

"Vodka, if you have it, please," I said. "I'm 18."

He winked as though he already knew I was lying.

"Ok, 14," I conceded.

We smoked and drank until the early hours. When we finally staggered outside and began to sober up, my mates began to panic.

"We're going to be in so much trouble when we get home," said one.

"I'm grounded for a month, and that's if I'm lucky," another said.

I was panicking too, but not about being in trouble with my parents. I was worried in case the little ones had woken in the night and needed me. I hated to think of Mum calling my name and me not replying. I had let them all down. Hurrying home, I was relieved to find Mum sleeping peacefully on the mattress, Dad dozing on the sofa nearby, the littles ones tucked up in the bunk beds. Nobody had even missed me. The next day, I went back to the same street in town, hoping the copper and his mate would be there. Again, back at their place, I was plied with booze and cigarettes. Through a drunken haze, I was aware of a squeeze of my knee, a kiss on my cheek, a hand brushing against my breast.

"You're gorgeous, Tara," they smarmed.

I hated it. Each time a hand came towards me I froze.

I gulped back more vodka to blot it out. Some nights, I couldn't wait to get away from the place and yet still, time after time, I went back. My need for approval and affection was visceral, and it trumped all else. One evening, maybe two months on, I turned up at their place in tears. There was no particular trigger for my despair, it was, as usual, a piling up of miseries, one after another, until I felt suffocated by the sheer volume.

Mum had been awake the previous night, sobbing as she relived Grampy's abuse. I'd got into a row with Dad when he flipped her mattress the next morning. There was nothing in for breakfast, not even a slice of bread, and the little ones went to school with an empty stomach. That upset me more than anything.

"Come in, Tara, whatever's the matter?" asked the supposed police officer as he answered the door.

I shrugged it off; I was too ashamed of my family to admit what was going on. Instead, I drank even more than usual.

"Can I stay here tonight?" I asked. "I don't want to go home. Can't face it."

"Sure," they smiled.

As we watched TV, I felt a hand snaking around my shoulder. Another one on my leg. I saw a sudden image of Grampy, snapping open his cans of lager and grunting as he settled himself on the sofa. Repulsed, I gagged.

"I need the bathroom," I spluttered.

I dashed upstairs, leaving the door unlocked as I took deep

breaths to calm myself down. As I was splashing my face with cold water, I felt the police officer squeezing himself against me, his breath on my ear. Spinning me round to face him, he suddenly thrust his hand between my legs and pinned me against the sink. He was so close, I could see the hairs up his nose, the red lines running across his sclera.

"Please, no," I stuttered. "No!"

As his mouth came towards mine, I recoiled, managing to kick his shin as I wriggled out from under his arm. I fled the house in my bare feet and without my coat, sobbing as I ran the whole way home.

Even before I reached my street, I was blaming myself. What else had I expected? I had gone round there, 20, maybe 30 times and allowed them to fill me with alcohol. I was foolish to think they would expect nothing in return. This was all my own fault.

I didn't go back to the house again. But that didn't stop my search for paternal love and approval. I needed validation from others to shore up my own lack of self-belief. Round at Sammy's one night, I was invited back to the house of a man twice my age. Not long after my first drink, I began to feel dizzy and nauseous. In alarm, I realised my vision was blurring.

"What have you given me?" I slurred.

I wanted to get up to leave but couldn't seem to co-ordinate my arms and legs. I could barely keep my eyes open. All night, I drifted in and out of consciousness, aware of voices around me, hands on me, moist breath on the side of my neck. When I came round again, it was 5am.

"I need to get home," I gasped. "I have to take my little sisters to school."

All the way home, I retched and heaved. When I staggered in through the front door, I was surprised to see Dad in the hallway. He took one look at me and hit me clean in the face with a punch. When I regained consciousness, my face was pressed against the floorboards. Nobody asked how I was or where I had been. Somehow, I dragged myself up to bed and stayed there for 24 hours. I was not well enough even to look after my siblings. How was it, I wondered wearily, that I had fallen prey to yet another predator? Did they operate in packs, like rats, passing titbits of information from one to the next? Why me? Dad poked his head around my door that night and said, "That will teach you."

But of course it didn't. I was addicted to pain and suffering. I put myself in dangerous situations, not because they thrilled me, but because I thought that was all I was worth. I needed so desperately to be loved – or even to be noticed – and I didn't know how else to go about it.

10

FOR ALL the changes in my teenage years, my new-found defiance was the most striking and it grew more intense as the months passed. From being a child who rarely spoke, I became a teenager who was permanently looking for a fight. There was an angry flint under the surface, always ready to ignite. I got into trouble at school for arguing with teachers or defending my siblings against bullies. I had screaming arguments with my father. I was constantly annoyed with my family, my teachers, the social workers and the police. And, most of all, with myself.

The changes were not without benefits. From being exiled by my peers, I was suddenly the envy of many. Whilst they rushed home for curfews and rules, I was a free spirit. Nobody missed me when I was gone. My only concern, and this was self-imposed, was looking after Mum and my younger siblings.

I had a ready supply of cash, lifted easily from Dad's pockets or the £10 notes which littered our living room. And I had easy access to drugs too; something which my teenage friends could only dream of. Where once I'd been scorned, now I was included and popular in certain circles. Kids I barely knew would ask me for a wrap of amphetamine or a block of weed.

"Your mum is so cool," they said. "No rules, no punishments, and you have loads of drugs. You don't even have to go to school. You've no idea how lucky you are."

"No," I replied drily. "You're right. I don't."

My weekend visits to Grampy gradually petered out, as I began seeing my friends and hanging around with all the wrong people, though of course Grampy had been the worst of them all. But on rainy Saturday nights, looking for somewhere to drink underage without judgement, we sometimes ended up at his house.

Again, it is unfathomable to me, looking back, that I willingly went back there with my mates. It was about more than free booze too. I needed to smooth things over and pretend, to myself and to everyone else, that nothing bad had happened. Because the alternative was unthinkable. As with my mother, my friends thought Grampy was marvellous. He was generous with his cans of lager, and if the snap of each ring-pull sent shivers down my spine, nobody seemed to notice. He cracked jokes and told stories from his army days.

"Your Grampy is so sweet," my friends said. "We love him."

Inevitably, after a few drinks, his eyes and his hands began to wander.

"Ignore him," I told them. "Just tell him to get lost."

I couldn't begin to tell them the truth.

"Oh, he's just trying it on, that's what old blokes are like when they have a drink," said one of my friends.

I was, for a moment, blindsided. Was this simply a case of overstepping the mark? Were those years of abuse and suffering symptomatic of an old man blurring the boundaries? I no longer knew. One night, I went round with three or four friends and Grampy was stocked up on lager and crisps. He'd been drinking already and was unsteady even as he reached out for a welcome hug. I glared and side-stepped it.

I felt uneasy as Grampy snapped open can after can, grunting softly as his gaze travelled over my friends. Under the TV was a treacherous stack of videos: 'Elvis on tour,' 'The Best of Elvis,' 'Eastenders Omnibus.' I shuddered. This whole place was teeming with deceit. The lies dripped from the walls and ran, like a sewer, under the floorboards. Whilst Grampy and my friends chatted, I tuned out, gazing at the shutter door at the end of the room. I remembered how it had closed of its own accord when I was small.

"That's the demons," Grampy had told me, and I'd inched closer to him, anxious to feel the warmth of his protection.

I knew now who the demon was. And he was sitting on the same sofa as me. Grampy stood to bring more drinks and one of my friends got up to use the bathroom. Grampy seemed to fall into her, lunging, with both hands grabbing her breasts.

"Grampy!" I screamed. "Stop it! Leave her alone!"

She was shaken, though she tried to laugh it off as we left.

"I'm sorry," I told her. "He's a perv. You really have to keep an eye on him."

By the time we reached the bus stop, my friends were joking about Grampy, making excuses because he was drunk and dismissing him as a harmless old man. I stayed tight-lipped. I couldn't bear to tell them the whole story. As a little girl, I had longed for friendship. But even now, surrounded by girls my own age, I could not bring myself to confide in anyone. I wore a cloak of shame so thick and heavy nobody could get close. Emotionally and physically, I kept people away. I didn't allow anyone inside my family home. I had built a barrier between me and the rest of the world, and nobody could pull it down – not even me.

Although I was surrounded by friends, family and peers, I was unbearably lonely. Despite the make-up and the racy outfits, I hated myself now more than ever. My diary had vanished at some point after I turned 14. Dad had always liked to make fun of it, even though he was the one who had bought it. I had a sneaking suspicion he may have thrown it away out of spite, and with that, those records of my childhood soul-searching were gone forever. Now instead of scrawling in my diary, I spent my spare time staring into the bathroom mirror, finding fault with my reflection. I was self-conscious about my teenage acne. My nose was bent out of shape, from the time Dad hit me. I decided I was too fat;

a dysmorphic symptom, because I never ate enough to be overweight. I'd been slim, or even thin, all my life. Regardless, I began limiting my calories, which wasn't especially difficult in a house where food was scarce. I pinched amphetamine from my mother too, just dipping my finger in, here and there, to suppress my appetite.

"If I was just a bit thinner, I'd be prettier," I told Cassie. "I might get a nice boyfriend instead of all these perverts I keep attracting."

Yet deep down, this was nothing to do with losing weight. Stopping eating gave me control over my life, in the same way that cleaning gave my mother control over hers. As the weeks passed, I lost a few pounds, and I became gaunt and skinny. Yet still, I looked in the mirror and hated what I saw. Too ugly. Too spotty. Too fat.

One night, Mum announced she was off to see a friend, a heroin addict, who lived at the other side of town.

"Can I come?" I asked.

I was desperate to get out of the house.

"Yes," she agreed. "But we'll be back very late, so you'll have to stay off school tomorrow."

"Fine by me," I beamed.

I hardly went to school anyway. Off we went arm in arm to the bus stop, and I convinced myself this was a pleasant mum and daughter outing, a bonding session. Mum and her friend disappeared into the kitchen, and I was told to stay in the living room. It grew late and, bored, I drifted off to sleep on the sofa. Sometime later, I woke with a jolt to find the room in darkness and two eyes staring into mine, our noses almost touching. I shot up with a blood curdling scream.

"Mum!" I yelled. "Mum! There's a man!"

The man watched in silence as I grabbed my shoes and coat, still screaming for my mother. He was the biggest man I had ever seen. He had broad, angular shoulders and seemed to fill the room. As I was rushing to the front door, Mum's friend appeared at the top of the stairs.

"Your Mum went home hours ago," she said. "She must have forgotten about you."

The man was behind me as I hurried out into the deserted street and started to run. I had no idea if he was following me as I raced through the darkness, my heart bursting out of my chest. Every now and again, gasping for breath, I dared to slow down and check over my shoulder. There was nobody there, but in the darkness, I convinced myself I saw his great, hulking outline hurtling towards me. By the time I arrived home almost an hour later, the sky was pink with a new day. Most of my fear had dissipated through sheer exhaustion. I tiptoed past Mum, asleep on her mattress, and then, even then, I could not find it in my heart to blame her. I was furious with the rest of the world, but never with her. I looked at her face and saw a damaged child. In her, I saw myself.

Into my final year at high school, my attendance stood at a measly 12%. Now that I was 15, the social workers and teachers seemed less involved than ever. If anything, they seemed relieved not to have me at school; I was a problem they could not fix. The truancy lady had given up on our family years earlier. All it took was for Dad to rage at her through the doorway one morning to frighten her off. We never saw her after that.

This was a pattern within the agencies who should have helped us. People didn't come to our house more than once or twice because Dad would fly into a temper and chase them down the street. As a result, I was never able to forge a connection with anyone and I trusted nobody. I am unsure, looking back, whether Dad's behaviour was a deliberate ploy to stop me being able to build relationships and confide my secrets, or more likely, whether he just could not control his temper.

Regardless, the lack of support, and certainly the lack of continuity, made me feel lonelier than ever. I diverted my frustrations and began shoplifting, partly because I needed things, but mostly to make a silent statement to the world. There was a chemist shop opposite the school gates, and, on the rare days I attended, I nipped in to steal something. Some mornings, I'd help myself to a lipstick or a mascara. Other times, it might be a hair scrunchie or a nice shower gel. I had little insight and even less remorse; in my mind, the owner of the chemist shop belonged in the same shameful group of adults as Grampy, Dad and the agencies who let me down on a daily basis. I was aggrieved by them all.

"Where did you get that hair slide, Tara?" my friends asked. "It's nice."

"Mum got it for me," I said proudly. "I've got a whole set in different colours."

So whilst my schoolwork suffered, my shop-lifting skills were perfected. I stole sanitary pads, spot cream and perfume. I branched out into other shops and got myself a new pencil case with stationery. I stole little trinkets for my younger siblings too. Was I slowly metamorphosing into my mother? The idea thrilled and appalled me in equal measure. One afternoon, I played truant and went into town with some friends to steal clothes. Buoyed by a teenage arrogance of never having been caught, I helped myself to a new outfit and some jewellery. I was just on my way out of the store when I felt a tap on my shoulder.

"Can you come this way, please?" asked a security guard.

Shamefaced, me and my friends handed over our haul and a police officer arrived.

"We need to call your parents," he announced.

We all froze in panic, though mine was a different variety than my friends. They were frightened of getting in trouble with their parents whereas I was doubtful my parents would even respond or care.

"You can call my grandfather," I said, reeling off the number.

With his army background and his façade of respectability, I thought Grampy would be unimpressed by my behaviour.

But then, I was unimpressed by his. As only a teenager can, I found a small advantage in a bleak situation. Like the lager and crisps, like the Jaffa cakes and the chocolate teacakes, I accepted the measly crumbs which fell into my lap, because otherwise, what was there for me? Grampy filled in some forms in the manager's office and afterwards, we got the same bus home. To my surprise, he seemed amused by my arrest.

"That's my girl," he chuckled, as we waited at the bus stop.

I didn't want praise for doing something wrong, yet it was better than no praise at all, and I was irritated to find myself smiling with him.

"We won't mention the shoplifting to your parents or anyone else," he continued, as though he was doing me a big favour.

The fuse lit, I suddenly rounded on him furiously.

"I know you won't mention it and we both know why," I snapped. "Don't speak to me, don't look at me and don't ever touch me."

I got off the bus leaving Grampy staring awkwardly into the distance. Slowly, I was beginning to understand the manipulation; how he dropped compliments, like fairy dust into boiling oil, to confuse me and bind me to him. The control and grooming were as unforgivable as the abuse itself. Yet I had little time to dwell on Grampy's behaviour because arriving home after my shoplifting expedition was like stepping into a cyclone. Mum's state of mind seemed, if anything, to be getting worse, and I found her on the mattress sobbing and wailing incoherently. Her instability was raw and terrifying, and I worried that one day, I might not be able to give her the comfort she needed.

"Where have you been?" she asked me reproachfully. "I've been waiting for you all day, Tar. I can't stop thinking about what he did to me. I can't live with it, I really can't."

I cradled her head, as my own threatened to burst in confusion, and I tried to separate the details of her abuse from my own. But how could I split these two traumas, when we shared the same perpetrator? As I lived through Mum's agony, I relived my own.

I wanted her to confide in me, and I treasured that bond we shared. Yet I was no longer so sure that this was a sign of her love for me or that I was the lucky one. The load weighed me down, as though I was carrying rocks in my pockets. It was so heavy and there was nobody to share it. I had been raised with the conviction that I could somehow fix and heal my family. But I was beginning to see it was both a crippling responsibility and a hopeless task.

"Mum, this isn't your fault," I whispered, smoothing her damp hair back from her face. "You cannot blame yourself."

Never, at any point, was there an opportunity for me to share my own mirror-image troubles with her. So many times, I tried to tell her. I tried mumbling the first few lines, to test the water.

'Can I talk to you about Grampy, Mum?'

Or I burst into tears, and ran to her for comfort, hoping she would ask what the matter was. But she never did. She never seemed to notice my distress. Or perhaps she saw it and turned away. She could not, I reminded myself, cope with her own problems, never mind mine too. It was a struggle even to persuade her to help me with the smallest practical issue. My acne was, exacerbated by stress, getting worse and worse and I begged both of my parents, over and over, to come with me to the GP.

"You don't need to do anything, just sit there and agree with what they prescribe," I said.

I'd already been to the doctor myself, only to be told I needed a parent with me before they would make a referral. I made several appointments, none of which we kept, because Dad was always in a bad mood and Mum was always too tired.

"Please, Mum, please," I pleaded.

Each morning, when I checked the bathroom mirror, I noticed a new spot. It felt like they were invading, taking over my whole face, working against me, just like everyone else. One day, I broke down sobbing. I'd had enough. Reaching for a bottle of bleach, I tipped it onto my bare hands and wiped them across my cheeks. The agony was almost euphoric as the bleach burned and stung. In some strange way, this felt like a step forward.

"Look at my face," I told Mum. "Now will you come to the doctors with me please?"

Even she could not fail to notice the raw patches and blisters across my skin.

"Okay," she agreed.

Later that week, the GP suggested a referral to a specialist. I was over the moon as we left. Now, at last, I would get help.

"Thanks, Mum," I beamed, linking my arm in hers. I clung to these small and rare kindnesses from her; they were bursts of sunshine for my soul and I collected them like a magpie gathering shiny treasures. Each morning, I waited for the postman, hoping he'd bring my letter from the hospital. The weeks passed and nothing arrived, and though the wounds from the bleach cleared up, my spots did not.

"Has anyone seen my letter?" I asked, sorting through junk on the table. "It's important."

Nobody replied but out of the corner of my eye, I caught sight of a scrap of paper inside the bong dad was building. Leaning in, I read out the address of The Great Western Hospital.

"That's my letter!" I gasped. "That's my hospital letter!"

Dad had shredded my letter, using it as a mixer for his drugs.

"How could you?" I sobbed, as he shrugged and lit a match.

I watched, helplessly, as my hopes burned along with his drugs. The next day, filled with determination, I went into school. Instead of going to my lessons, I found a support teacher who had helped me in the past. As I recounted the story of my hospital referral, her eyes filled with sympathy.

"Let's see if I can help," she said.

I waited whilst she called the hospital and, after lengthy explanations, she ended the call with a smile.

"You have an appointment, the week after next," she told me. "And don't worry, I will take you there myself."

Roaccutane, the doctor warned, carried with it a risk of depression. I already knew this, I had researched it thoroughly myself, and I waved away his concerns.

"I'm already depressed," I told him. "I'll be even worse if you don't let me have this drug. Please, just give me a chance."

He pointed out that my spots were a symptom, and not a cause, of my stress. But I had thought about that too.

"I know the spots are not the real problem," I conceded. "I can't change the stress in my life. But I can change the spots."

We walked out of the hospital with a prescription, and a promise that I would return for a check-up. My teacher seemed almost as pleased as I was.

"Thanks, Miss," I said.

I was still beaming when she dropped me back at home. I couldn't understand why anyone would be so nice to me. I don't remember her name, or her face. But I will never forget her kindness. It means a lot to me, even today.

11

MY SKIN improved slowly but my mental state, as the doctor had warned, remained low. Several times a week, I drank with the sole purpose of blacking out, always frustrated and bitter when I came round later.

"Why am I still here?" I asked angrily. "Why do I have to go through this, again and again?"

My mantra: 'Tomorrow will come', suddenly felt like a cruel joke, turned completely on its head, because I did not want a tomorrow. I no longer wanted to be a part of this world and the phrase felt like more of a threat than a promise. Those nights, drinking in the local park or at the bus stop, I was so jealous of my peers. By 10pm, their phones were bleeping with text messages from caring parents: 'Where are you? You have school tomorrow. Time to come home.'

I longed for a call like that. I ached for someone to miss me, to care about me, to be anchored within the solid framework of a family. I would have loved to have been grounded for arriving home drunk or coming in too late. But the truth was, my parents didn't even notice when I was out, never mind worry about what time I might be back. I needed to be home to look after my younger siblings and to check on Mum. But the concern, sadly, flowed only one-way. Some evenings, if the weather was bad or we had no money, we ended up hanging out at Grampy's house. We knew we could rely on a steady supply of White Lightning cider, but we also knew it came at a price.

My friends understood to keep their distance from his wandering hands, and they sniggered quietly at his dirty jokes and delusional claims of the women he'd slept with. They didn't realise it went any further than that. But as I listened to his ridiculous stories, my face was frozen, unable to fake a smile. My thoughts were so dark. So bleak. Grampy continued to fill and refill my glass with cider. Why? It was as though he was trying to knock me over the edge, to shove me into a bottomless abyss. It would certainly suit him if I drank myself to death, taking with me his filthy secrets.

He already knew my mother would never have the strength to stand up to him. I was the problem. I was the fly in his ointment. On the outside, I continued as normal; I did the school run with my siblings, I cooked, I washed and I cleaned. I laughed and gossiped with my friends. I drank worrying quantities of cider. But inside, I was drenched with despair. I was drowning in it. And as was the way in my family, just as I thought life could get no worse, it did. I came home one night to find Mum sobbing over a letter informing her she needed to appear in court on drugs charges.

"You'll be okay," I told her. "Don't worry."

She had appeared before Swindon magistrates several times in the past, either for drug offences or non-payment of fines. It was never usually seen as a big deal. But this time, it was different.

"This is serious, Tar," she cried. "I've had too many warnings. I will go down this time. I know I will."

I continued to comfort her. It seemed impossible that Mum could go to prison for any length of time. She was, in my eyes, too naïve and fragile to even answer these charges. Her lifestyle jarred sharply with her character; the two sides of her scraped together side by side like sandpaper; the innocent nine-year-old, whose development was squashed by her father's rapes, squabbling for position with the worn-out 36-year-old drug addict.

"You'll be okay," I told her again.

On the day of her court hearing, I was up earlier than usual. Dad took the little ones to school whilst I made sure Mum was up and dressed on time. I called school and pretended to be her, letting them know I was off sick – again. Nobody questioned it. We didn't pack an overnight bag because that felt too pessimistic. But Mum was uncharacteristically quiet on the bus journey there. I took her hand, but it felt limp and cold in mine. When we arrived at the courthouse, I hugged her and said, "I'll be right outside waiting for you."

She went to sign in with the court staff, and I took my place in the public gallery. Much of what happened in the hearing passed me by. I focused solely on Mum's face, on the way her fingers twisted together and the way her big eyes filled with tears. It felt so wrong, as though one of my little sisters was in the dock. Or even my own child.

"I sentence you to nine months imprisonment," the judge announced.

With a jolt, I snapped back to reality. My heart hammered against my chest as Mum was led away, by security staff, to the cells.

"She doesn't even have her overnight bag," I cried out, as the tears poured down my face. "No pyjamas, no toothbrush!"

No drugs, I wanted to add. She would miss those more than anything. But I kept that to myself.

"Please, don't take her away!" I sobbed.

But she was gone. I staggered outside and continued crying all the way home on the bus. And soon, my sorrow was displaced by worry. Panic rushed like a hurricane through me. Not: 'What would I do without my mother?' but: 'What would she do without me?' I knew she would not cope on her own. Dad was waiting when I arrived home. Seeing him, my anxiety quickly liquidised into molten fury.

"This is your fault!" I yelled. "Those drugs belonged to you. Why did you let her take the blame? Why do you never look after her?"

"I am a better parent than your mum," Dad yelled back.

"She can't look after kids, and I can. So she has to take the rap. Simple."

I stared at him in disbelief.

"A better parent!" I scoffed. "You have to be joking. You're useless. You are no kind of father."

I knew I had gone too far but I didn't care. I didn't even feel any pain as Dad manhandled me out of the front door before slamming it in my face.

"And don't think you're coming back in here tonight," he bawled through the living room window.

I wandered around outside for a while until it started to rain. I had no choice but to go to Grampy's, there was nowhere else. He was, as usual, pleased to see me. How was it that the only person in the world who welcomed me was the same person who was trying to destroy me? How was it that I was reliant on my abuser? Had he made me that way, was that his plan from the start? Already drunk himself, Grampy produced a bottle of White Lightning for me. The last thing I needed was alcohol, yet Grampy seemed determined to see me finish the bottle.

"Drink up," he slurred, slopping more cider into my glass.

I felt sick with unease. He was pushing me, insidiously, to my limit. I was so lost, so lonely. And so close to the edge that I felt the ground crumbling beneath my feet. I knew that, and I think Grampy knew that too. I wanted him to ask me about the court hearing and to commiserate over Mum. But he barely reacted when I told him she was in prison. He was too drunk to follow my conversation, too eaten up by his own problems to hear mine. Early the next morning, I was back home before the school run. Dad held a grudge only as long as it suited him, and he needed help with the little ones. The reality of Mum being gone started to sink in as my siblings pointed out the empty mattress.

"Where's Mum?" they frowned.

"She'll be back soon," I sighed. "Now come on, get your shoes on."

I had always mothered them on a practical level. But with Mum gone, the responsibility weighed more. Everything was on me. Everything was my job. There were such great expectations of me, and they were so unwieldy. I felt less able to cope, to step into the role, than ever before. My mind was swollen with worry over how Mum was, if she was eating, if she was safe.

"I need to visit her," I told Dad. "Please, let me see her."

"You can't," he told me.

Most nights, I cried myself to sleep. I was always trying to lose weight but suddenly I found I had no appetite at all. My days were so fraught that I had no time for school. One morning, I came back from the school run to find a support worker waiting in our living room. I knew Dad would be furious if I spoke up but also realised this could be my only chance.

"Can I see my mother?" I asked. "Please?"

Dad began to object but the support worker interrupted

him and said, "The girl needs to see her mother. It might help them both."

"Thank you," I mumbled, suddenly shy. I didn't know how to react. I wasn't used to being noticed, less still accommodated.

The next time I saw the support worker, she had arranged a visit to Eastwood Park prison in Gloucestershire. She even offered to drive me there. I was beside myself with nervous excitement all the way, pleased to see Mum but worried about what state she'd be in. The support worker said very little on our long journey, leaving my mind to wander. I imagined Mum with black eyes and bruises, singled out and picked on by the prison bullies. I wondered if she was eating okay. She was already stick-thin; she couldn't afford to lose any more weight. At the prison, an officer approached me to pat me down in a search.

Immediately, I was thrust back to my bedroom and the assault by the police officer. Again, I felt those cold fingers under my t-shirt. Closing my eyes, I braced myself for a sexual assault. Even though I was in a public place, surrounded by people, this was what I expected. This was what I had been raised to expect. I was worth nothing more.

"All done, love," the officer smiled, as she patted my pockets. "In you go."

I sagged with relief as I walked into the visiting hall. I felt as though I had somehow got away lightly. Raising my head, I spotted Mum immediately, and my heart was warm with love.

"Tar!" she called.

Walking closer, I was momentarily caught between happiness at seeing my mother and shock at her appearance. Her eyes were bright, and her hair was freshly cut, shiny and thick. She had gained weight, and her face had filled out a little. It suited her. I had never seen her look so healthy.

"Mum!" I gasped.

I wanted to hug her but wasn't sure it was allowed. And it was awkward, taking my place next to the support worker, us on one side of a small table, Mum on the other. I was knocked a little off balance by her appearance, and I couldn't be myself with a stranger listening in to our conversation.

"Mum, you look great," I said eventually.

"I feel it," she beamed. "I like it in here. It's doing me good."

Again, I reeled in shock. I had expected her to weep; to tell me how much she missed me. I was pleased, of course, that she seemed so happy. Yet the affirmation stung. Did she not miss me, the way I missed her? Conversely, I felt like I was the one serving the sentence. My own days were filled with worry and stress, looking after the littles ones and dodging Dad's tempers. Whilst Mum was blooming, I was skinny and gaunt. I hadn't had a good night's sleep in weeks.

"I've met so many new mates in here," Mum told me. "Really nice girls, you know?"

I didn't but I nodded numbly.

"And this will cheer you up," she smiled. "Guess what? No drugs in here, Tar. I've not touched them in months."

Now it was my turn to laugh and whoop with joy. I almost forgot the support worker was next to me as I clapped my hands.

"Really?" I pressed. "Really? Do you promise?"

"I'm clean!" she yelled, flinging out her arms and titling back her head. The action was so child-like and innocent. I could almost forget we were in a prison hall. I had been dreading our goodbye, but it was softened by the news that she was drug-free. Driving home, the support worker was again completely silent, yet I could not stop smiling. This, I told myself, must be how other kids felt on Christmas morning.

I allowed myself to envisage a new future, one where Mum would be a real mother, a normal mother. There would be no more drugs, no more strangers calling, no more police raids. She would stand up to Dad, maybe even leave him, move house, start afresh. There would be no more secrets. I leaned my head against the passenger window and closed my eyes as I was carried away on a marshmallow cloud of daydreams.

Like all other adults charged with our care, the support worker mysteriously vanished after the prison visit. Dad and his unpredictable temper saw to that. Still, I was not especially concerned. Now that I had seen Mum, and witnessed her dramatic life-change, I felt new energy and purpose. I even returned to school part-time for those final two months of her sentence. In textiles, I made a cushion, shaped like

Eeyore, with 'Mum' embroidered across his front. On the day she was due for release, I finished off the final few stitches and carried it home, hardly daring to hope. As I reached our house, the bedroom window was flung open and the voice I loved shouted:

"Tar!"

Perhaps it was a trick of the late afternoon light, but in that moment, my mother sparkled and dazzled like an angel.

"Mum!" I squealed, dashing inside. "Oh, I've missed you. Look how pretty you are! You look great!"

She looked, if anything, even better than the last time. She laughed as we hugged and I watched, amazed, as her whole face transformed. It was, I realised, the first time she had ever smiled with her eyes. I had never seen her like this; it was almost like meeting Mum for the first time; meeting the woman she could and should have been, if abuse and drugs had not dragged her down.

"I'm clean," she told me.

I knew she was telling me the truth. The proof shone out of her.

"I'm so proud of you," I said, tears of happiness spilling onto her cushion. "Don't ever leave me again. Promise me."

I had dreamed so many times of our reunion, and it was a million times better than I could have imagined. It was so wonderful to have her home. Our family was complete. And yet in some ways, it was like welcoming a stranger into the fold. I was meeting my mother, my true mother, for the first time. Mum helped me to get the little ones into bed, and as she was tucking them in, I heard voices downstairs.

"Just a few of your Dad's mates," she shrugged casually. "They've come round to welcome me home."

"No," I stuttered. "Not them. It's their fault you were in prison in the first place."

"Oh, Tar, it'll be fine," she said.

I wanted to believe her, but my skin was tight with anxiety. Mum went downstairs, and soon the smell of cannabis wafted up into the bedrooms. I crept down and watched at the living room door, my heart plunging as she prepared herself a line of drugs on the edge of the table.

"Mum! You promised me!" I wailed. "You promised!"

"Oh," she said vaguely, turning towards me. "I'm not back on it. I'm just celebrating. This is different. Come on, Tar, let me enjoy my first night at home."

She was like a small child, pleading for a later bedtime.

"This is a one-off," she told me, in a way that suggested she didn't even believe it herself.

Without doubt, she was lost to me again. That afternoon, those few short hours filled with promise and potential, were as precious as they were painful. I met my real mother that afternoon. But I would never see her again. It would become an unreachable memory, like a lost photograph. If only Mum could have seen how she looked that day; the way she held herself, how the light caught her hair, the sparkle in her eyes. She radiated hope. But it was all gone.

"I'm just celebrating," she mumbled, as I started to cry. "Give me a break."

The light drained from her even as she spoke and she sagged like the Eeyore cushion, now lost amongst clouds of smoke. As my heart shattered, my temper surged.

"I can't do this any more!" I yelled. "I can't keep cleaning up after you. I'm just a kid myself. I can't take any more broken promises."

I was furious with Dad for not showing more restraint and support. And, despite myself, I was angry with Mum for crumbling so easily. In bed, I pulled the pillow over my ears to drown out the laughter downstairs and the inevitable arguments which would follow. My ephemeral pride in my mother drained away like dirty dishwater down a plug hole. It was so sad how people damaged themselves. It was sadder still how they damaged others.

12

I WAS, for many months, deeply distressed by Mum's failure to stay clean, and more so, by her failure to even try. Her transformation had lasted less than a day. In some ways, I still feel that disappointment today. After her spell in prison, Mum deteriorated quickly, she seemed to fall headlong back into drugs and depression, worse even than before.

I saw her disintegration as a warning, and the bells clanged in my head more loudly than ever. I was missing school, hanging around until the early hours of the morning, drinking, smoking and taking drugs. Much as I adored my mother, I did not want to end up like her. As had always been the way throughout my life, when I reached the point of absolute peril, self-preservation kicked in. I was no more than a casual drug user, but I stopped taking them completely.

I cut down on alcohol and began eating as sensibly and healthily as I could, given my home environment. My school attendance was poor; some days I was too busy looking after my siblings or Mum, and my education was an inconvenience, an irritation. I didn't for a minute think I'd be able to go onto further education, or I'd ever get a good job. My self-esteem was so low, I really didn't think I was capable. Who on earth would put their faith in a girl like me? I was, however, keen to make my own way in life and determined to break the family mould.

My own parents were, sadly, an example of what not to be. I did not judge them; I did not even blame them. They had their own burdens. But I knew my life had to be different than theirs. One Saturday morning, I got up early and went down to the market in the town centre. By the time I came home, I had a part-time job. To my knowledge, I was the first person in my family to have ever been employed. I was certainly the only one in the house earning a wage.

"You've done what?" Dad spluttered, when I made my announcement.

"I've got a job at the food market," I said. "Friday nights and Saturday mornings."

"Why?" he asked, genuinely stunned. "What's the matter with you?"

He and Mum were at a loss. And, as the news sunk in, their shock crystallised into resentment.

"Why do you have to be different?" Dad snapped. "You think you're better than us, don't you? Well, you're not. You're a stuck-up cow. You're nothing."

The irony was galling. My self-esteem was at zero. I didn't think I was better than anyone at all. But I refused to let him see I was hurt.

"I'm not you," I snapped. "But I'm not nothing."

Even before my first week's wages landed, I had flicked through the Argos catalogue, ticking off imaginary purchases. I imagined a home filled with products from the pages of the catalogue and it became a little paradise in my head. I wanted to support myself; I strived towards a better life. How was that so wrong? My aspirations were not material but as a teenager, that was my only measuring stick. In truth, I longed only for peace, happiness and a life free from fear and abuse. And my job at the market was the first step on my journey. Mum fell pregnant late that year with her eighth child. I was about to do the school run one afternoon when I heard her yelling my name from the bathroom.

"Baby's coming!" she told me, surprisingly calm.

With a whoosh of panic and excitement, I realised I had no idea what to do.

"Breathe, breathe," I told her, grabbing her shoulders and copying a scene I'd watched on telly. "Breathe deeply."

I ran to call an ambulance and then went back to Mum. She was still on the toilet and, as I peered under her, I saw the baby's head.

"He's coming!" I gasped. "He's nearly here!"

With two more pushes, my baby brother slid out, into my waiting arms. I was dumbstruck, overcome with shock and love. Mum, on the other hand, had done this seven times before and was remarkably unfazed.

"Let's call him Louis," she joked, as the paramedics arrived to cut the cord.

Everyone laughed and, in that moment, I felt a surge of affection. She could be so funny; so warm and entertaining. And yet, even as I smiled, nascent worries skittered through my mind. How would she cope with another baby? Or more accurately, how would I cope? The social workers would be round soon to inspect us all. They might take our new baby away.

If not him, then one of the others. The anxiety was a stodgy lump in my throat and soon, I found I could not laugh at all. Mum and my baby brother were both taken to hospital and, because he was small, the doctors wanted to admit them both. But Mum wouldn't hear of it. Though she'd just given birth, she was still feisty and fiery. She and the baby were allowed home after she agreed to daily visits from the midwives and health visitor. Baby Cameron, as he was eventually named, was beautiful.

"I'm here for you, sweetheart," I told him, as I rocked him to sleep.

But I knew I could not raise him myself. My family had always been the central structure around which I had rigidly built my life. But not anymore. For my own sanity, I needed to distance myself. One evening, hanging around with my mates, I got talking to a man named Jude, who looked just like Tom Cruise. I had just turned 16, he was four years older and I fell for him that same night. He was my first love and I was besotted. When I fell pregnant, soon after, we were both shocked. But whilst Jude was a little rattled by the prospect of giving up his freedom, I embraced it.

I became obsessed with the notion of becoming a mother, of having a baby to love and love me back. In my head, I created an idyllic life, with my own baby and my own home. The pregnancy became my salvation. My baby was my lifeline, just as I was theirs. I dreaded telling my parents, not because I thought they'd be angry or shocked, but because I feared they would have no reaction at all. And I was right.

"I'm having a baby," I announced.

Neither of them really acknowledged my news. They were hostage to their demons and too engrossed in their own problems to listen to me. But I was confident I could manage on my own, even at 16. I had never relied on anyone else, and I was not about to start. As my bump began to show, I liked resting a hand on my belly and feeling the love running osmotically from my fingertips into the baby. The connection was already there.

I talked every day to my baby, making promises and plans, deliberating over names and picking out prams and highchairs in my trusty Argos catalogue. It didn't matter that I couldn't afford them yet; I knew I would cope somehow. I felt more settled and surer of myself than ever before. The midwife handed out free vouchers, and I felt a thrill of excitement every time I bought a packet of nappies or wipes or a tiny pair of white socks. I stored everything in a drawer at

Jude's house. It felt wrong somehow, to keep baby clothes at my own house. I didn't want something so delicate and pure polluted by drugs. At 16 weeks, I had a scan which showed I was carrying a little girl. Jude and I decided to call her Acacia.

"Acacia," I whispered, over and over, rolling the name around my mouth. I loved it. A couple of weeks later, I was called in for a routine appointment at the hospital. Waiting at the bus stop with Jude, my antenatal file in my arms, I swelled with pride. This was the start of a new chapter for us all. But as I leaned on the bus shelter, I slowly became aware of a dull ache in my lower abdomen.

"I don't feel well," I told Jude. "I think I need to lie down."

His house was nearer than mine and by the time we got inside, there was a gush of blood running down the side of my leg. Suddenly, I was catapulted back to the age of seven. I was trapped in Grampy's bathroom, staring at the blood in the water. Dizzy and nauseous, I held onto Jude for balance.

"Tara," he said, snapping me back to reality. "You're bleeding."

I lay on the sofa and tried to blink away the image from my childhood. Was this an omen that my baby might not survive? Was this my punishment; abused as a child, I would never be allowed a child of my own? By the time the ambulance arrived, I was bleeding heavily. With the sirens blaring, and a horrible sadness in the pit of my stomach, I was rushed to hospital. I was examined and then a doctor said, "I'm very sorry, you've lost your baby."

I'd known it deep down, but the confirmation was an axe through my heart.

"I'll call your family, let them know," Jude told me, as he said goodbye.

I was wheeled into a side ward and, as I lay back on the pillow, I felt another stab of pain. The bed was soaked with a second haemorrhage as I slipped into unconsciousness. I was vaguely aware of a nurse pressing the buzzer by my bed and a crowd of medics rushing around me. When I woke, I'd had surgery.

"You have been through quite a scare," the doctor told me. "You need lots of rest."

But I didn't care about myself. I just wanted my baby girl. My Acacia. Alongside my grief, I felt so angry with myself. I was furious that I had allowed myself to believe that something – anything – good might ever happen in my life. I was a fool to have dreamed that I could be normal. I was a failure. A joke. I could not keep myself safe – how on earth did I expect to keep a baby safe? I'd never forgive myself. I blamed my weight; perhaps I was too thin to carry a baby. Or maybe I'd caused my own miscarriage through stress. My mind whirred with accusations whilst my body struggled to recover from the trauma. Even after a blood transfusion, I was weak and exhausted. The following day, a nurse came to see me and asked me to sign some papers. The words blurred on the page as I wrote my name and address. I had no idea what I was signing.

"Your baby will be with all the other babies," she told me. "She won't be on her own."

I didn't know what she meant, and I didn't ask. I wanted to feel comforted that Acacia was not alone, but that just made her feel even further away from me. I was in hospital for one week and in that time, I didn't have a single visitor. Jude was young; I had not expected him to turn up with a clean nightie and a stack of magazines for me. And though I did not for a moment believe my parents would visit, their absence cut deep just the same.

They didn't even call the ward to check on me. Visiting times only emphasised the ache inside me; the lack of a heartbeat in my belly reflected by the absence of family at my bedside. I watched enviously as visitors brought grapes and smiles as they gathered around other patients. One of the nurses made a real fuss of me, giving me leftover sandwiches or extra pots of ice cream from the food trolley. She even brought a bunch of flowers left by someone else. But nothing could fill the void inside me. I felt numb and hollow and utterly hopeless. On the day I was discharged, the hospital staff called my parents.

"There's no way they'll come for me," I told them. "You're wasting your time."

"Well, we can't let you go home on your own," they replied.

Around lunchtime, Dad finally showed up on the ward.

The nurse who had befriended me marched over to confront him.

"Do you realise your daughter was in a bad way?" she asked him. "She's been in hospital for a week without any visitors."

If she thought she could shame Dad into an apology, she was sadly mistaken. He treated her with the same contempt he reserved for anyone who offered him advice, including me.

"I had to get two buses to get here," he told her irritably. "I don't know what your problem is."

He didn't seem to consider that we had to get two buses back also, and I really wasn't well enough to do the journey. Arriving back home, I felt desolate. The hospital had given me a small box with Acacia's name on the outside and a small teddy bear inside. It was all I had to remember her by – the only proof I had that she'd ever existed. Nobody ever mentioned her or said her name. Some days, I questioned whether I'd ever been pregnant at all. I didn't know where her remains were; if she'd been cremated or buried. I needed to grieve but didn't know what that grief looked like. I had lost a baby, a real person, a part of myself. Yet saying her name out loud felt wrong, as though I was supposed to be back to myself by now.

"Acacia," I whispered, with my head buried in my pillow. "Mummy loves you, darling."

As the months passed, I yearned for another baby. My

arms ached to hold a child in my arms. It was not about replacing Acacia or even about easing my grief. But I needed a focus for all the love and excitement I'd felt whilst I was carrying her. All those emotions had simply been sliced through without warning.

Now, they hovered inside me, expectantly. Though my first pregnancy had been a surprise I wanted, more than anything, to be a mother. As the months went on, my longings intensified. My friends had fancy watches, new outfits and designer trainers on their wish-lists. I had a baby on mine. But though I was desperate to fall pregnant, I found the act of sex itself very difficult. All intimacy reminded me of Grampy.

When I held Jude's hand, I saw Grampy's watch glinting on his wrist. I heard the horrible grunting sound Grampy made when he watched his filthy videos. Worst of all, I smelled that horrible stench in my nostrils; it was, for me, the smell of sex and always would be. Sex was inextricably linked with abuse, just as abuse was associated with love. And yet somehow, tragically, there was no connection between love and sex.

My view of relationships was badly twisted and damaged and perhaps irreparably so. I could not bear to use a tampon, and I could not contemplate oral sex, because of what had happened in Grampy's spare room. I could not even sleep in silence; I needed my birdsong. If there were no birds outside, I played a recording to lull me to sleep. And even then, I was plagued by nightmares which left me sweating and screaming. Jude soon worked out that my anxiety had sinister roots.

"I was abused when I was younger," I told him.

It ought to have been a seminal moment; this was the first time I'd said it loud. Instead, I brushed it off as something I needed to get out of the way quickly. I provided no details and nor did Jude press for any. I was not ready to tell him anything else, and I did not want pity. I'd never had attention as a child, and I didn't know how to cope with it. It was ironic that something I had longed for all those years was now the thing I shunned, because it scared me. Affection and sympathy were alien to me.

At the end of that year, I fell pregnant again. This time, because of the miscarriage, I was wary. And yet as the months passed, and my bump blossomed, I dared to hope. I had cravings for chilli sauce and I loved to see the changes in my body, day by day. Jude and I moved into our own flat, just a few minutes' walk from my family home, so I could go back daily to help with the little ones and to check on Mum. I got a new job, working at H Samuel jewellers in the town centre and saved hard, ready for our baby. I decorated the whole flat and bought cushions and lamps to make it homely. I bought the best baby equipment I could afford. I kept the place clinically clean and tidy. Behind it all, I was terrified of being judged because of my family's reputation. Sometimes, I worried that my surname alone might be enough for social services to step in and take my baby away.

"Is there anything else I need to do?" I asked my midwife. "Anything at all?"

"Tara, you're doing really well," she smiled. "You're going to be a good mum."

But the worry was like an itch under my skin and there was nothing I could do to ease it. One day, I was coming out of work when I spotted a big advert for Druglink, a charity offering help with addiction. I popped in, picked up a leaflet and took it straight round to show Mum.

"Will you give it a go?" I asked her. "They're offering acupuncture. You have never tried that."

"Can't," she shrugged. "I've nothing to wear. I haven't been out for weeks. I lost my shoes."

I was due to be paid the following week.

"I will buy you a coat and a pair of boots," I offered. "In return, please promise me you'll make an appointment."

She smiled, and in that moment, the whole room seemed to light up. There was an air of possibility, of anticipation.

"I promise," she agreed.

As soon as my wages landed, I kept my word. I turned up with Mum's new jacket and boots, and I booked her in with a counsellor. I took time off work to go with her, but when we arrived, the receptionist explained there'd been some sort of mix-up and asked Mum to come back the following day. It was too short notice for me to get more time off, but Mum promised she wouldn't let me down. On my break, the following afternoon, I quickly called home.

"How was it?" I asked.

"Oh," Mum mumbled. "I don't think I'm ready, Tar, really. Sorry. I didn't go in the end."

I felt more annoyed with myself than with her. There had been so many false dawns, so many broken promises. And yet, I just kept settling myself up for more heartbreak and more failure.

In August, two and a half weeks after my due date, I finally went into labour. At the hospital, delirious on gas and air, I was bewildered when a male doctor came into the room to examine me. In my confused mind, I convinced myself he was going to sexually assault me.

"No!" I yelled. "Leave me alone!"

As the midwife calmed me down, he rolled up his sleeves, and in his place, I saw Grampy, his own sleeves rolled, his cold eyes glinting from behind the lens of his glasses.

"No," I protested.

"Tara, it's OK," the midwife soothed. "We need to examine you because your labour isn't coming along as quickly as we'd like."

After the examination, a team of medics gathered around me. Suddenly alert, I cut through the haze. This was exactly what had happened when I miscarried Acacia.

"Am I losing my baby?" I asked in panic.

"The cord is around your baby's neck," the midwife explained. "We're taking you to theatre for a C-section."

Moments later, I was unconscious. When I awoke, and

dared to open my eyes, there he was. The most perfect little boy, sleeping in the cot beside me. My heart's desire.

"Hello, darling," I whispered. "I'm your Mummy."

That first cuddle was magical. Here was someone who needed me just the same as I needed him. I marvelled at his tiny nose, his rosebud mouth, his fingers splayed across my chest.

Ours was the purest love which grew and grew, moment by moment, until it filled my chest and bloomed like the world's most beautiful flower. Love pushed through the fissures and wounds in my soul and each time I looked at my baby, another crack was mended and another hurt was healed. I loved the feeling of his skin on mine. I had never had affection and wanted, so desperately, to transmit my devotion to my son.

With him in my arms, my world tilted and realigned in a different position, and I knew it would never be the same again. All my life I had been forced to keep secrets. But the joy of motherhood was the best kept and most wonderful secret of all, and I wanted to scream it from the rooftops. I smiled to myself at the assumption that teenage pregnancy ruins lives. Paradoxically, it had saved mine. I was euphoric. I was complete. I was loved. I called my baby Brandon and taking him home was both the proudest and most daunting moment of my life. All around me, I saw potential dangers. I worried I might drop him, panicked he might become ill, dreamed that he would stop breathing in the middle of the night.

Sometimes, I would wake and flick his cheek just to check he was breathing. The habit brought back horrific memories from Jasmine's drug overdose and the long night I had spent at her bedside, panicking she would die. Would I be allowed to keep my baby, given my family background? Would he be taken from me, either by the authorities or some higher power?

The irony that I might lose my own son, when for so many years my parents had evaded social services, was impossibly cruel. When the health visitor called me to arrange a visit, my skin grew tight with anxiety. Had she recognised my surname and assumed that I was trouble? I could not let myself believe it was merely a routine check. I had to prove myself, over and above any other parent. I cleaned the flat manically and yet as I scrubbed and disinfected, my thoughts drifted towards my mother. I remembered her ripping up carpets and throwing Shake n Vac around the place. Was I destined to end up like her?

"Tara, you are not good enough," I told myself. "You need to do more. You need to be more."

At my core, my belief in myself as a mother was solid. I had never felt so confident or engaged. Motherhood fit me snugly, like a second skin. But on the surface, my insecurities swirled like smog and my hormones made me question everything. Each visit with the health visitor and the midwife passed smoothly. I did not have a social worker; there was no need. And yet, still I worried. My need to protect Brandon went beyond the vigilance I'd shown towards my younger siblings. This was animalistic and it was visceral.

Like a mother lion, I would have clawed away anyone who tried to hurt him. So why, I asked myself, had my own mother not only failed to protect me, but placed me in the eye of the storm and left me there? I turned the facts over and over in my mind from all angles, but her behaviour was unforgiveable. Until now, I had always listened to Mum. This had been her story, and the confidences went one way only.

When I spoke, or tried to speak, of the abuse, it was in sugar-coated euphemisms. I might begin a sentence and trail off. I might cry, at her side, hoping she would ask what was wrong. I had never said it straight. But with my own son in my arms, I realised the time had come. I needed answers. In order to move forward as a mother myself, I had a right to know. I confronted her that same week.

"Grampy sexually abused me," I told her. "All through my childhood, again and again, I was abused."

Mum covered her face with her hands, and she did not look at me. My overwhelming urge was to comfort her, to soothe her, to swallow back my words. But I held back; I had a duty to my son to see this through.

"Why did you send me there?" I asked. "Why did you let me go? He had abused you and you must have known he would abuse me too."

"I didn't know, I didn't know," she sobbed, wringing her hands.

It tore me apart to see her cry, but I focused firmly, in my mind, on an image of my precious son.

"Even if you didn't know about the abuse, you knew there was a chance he'd abuse me," I said. "You sent me to the home of a paedophile. You knew what damage he did to you, yet you sent me there for the same."

Mum lifted her head to stare at me. She had no answer for this. My heart was heavy, but I pressed on.

"So, what are we going to do about it?" I asked. "We can't let him get away with this."

Mum shuddered and shook her head.

"He's too old. He's my dad," she wept. "I am sorry, Tar, but we can't go to the police, we have to keep it quiet. Promise me."

It was not the answer I wanted or deserved. But it was the one I expected. The little girl in me was counting on my mother to protect me. The adult knew she would not. She was soft and vulnerable and incapable of making a fair decision either for herself or for me. The conversation left me deflated and defeated, yet I did not regret it. It was pointless to confront my father. He had never once apologised to me or taken responsibility for anything, and I did not expect him to even acknowledge my suffering, let alone explain why he had let me visit the home of a paedophile throughout my childhood. Alongside the abuse, I had to shoulder the weight they had all placed on me. I had grown up listening to Grampy telling me I was special and hearing my mother say she would never cope without me. I had carried the hopes of my entire family on my young shoulders. I had thought I could fix them all. I saw now how utterly hopeless and misguided that was. Yes, I was the chosen one. But chosen for what, exactly?

13

THE BELIEF that I was not good enough to be a mother continued to roll over me like a thick fog. I loved Brandon fiercely and completely. But I felt so inadequate, so lacking. When he learned to sit up, aged six months, I bought him a little truck with bricks inside.

One afternoon, I sat on the carpet to teach him how to build a tower. Yet even though it was just the two of us, I felt self-conscious and uneasy, as though there was a hidden camera, recording my performance as a mother and judging all my mistakes. With a jolt, I realised I didn't really know how to play with Brandon. Nobody had ever played with me, and I had no experience at all of play. I felt such sadness that I was failing him. Battling my self-doubt, I signed up for a local parent and baby group.

On the playmat, with the other mums, I observed how they interacted with their children, and made mental notes. Later, at home, I reenacted what I had learned. I did my best, and Brandon certainly seemed to love it. He burst into peals of laughter as our tower of bricks fell over. But even then, as I collected the bricks, I felt like I was letting him down somehow. My lack of self-confidence was debilitating, and it was ruining everything, like picking up a lovely cupcake only to find black mould running underneath the icing. At my next appointment with the health visitor, she asked, "How are you managing, Tara? I know you're back home every day helping your mum and your younger siblings as well as looking after Brandon."

Perhaps if she had not offered an opening, I would have stayed quiet. Instead, it all spilled out; my fears that Brandon would be taken away, and my feelings of inadequacy and failure.

"You're a great mum," she said. "Nobody will take Brandon from you. We have no concerns at all. But you're a young mum and you have a lot to cope with."

She suggested I saw my GP who prescribed medication for postnatal depression. I was wary at first of taking tablets, but little by little the mist cleared, and I began to feel better. Without the constant worry that I might lose Brandon, I started to really enjoy motherhood. Each day, there was something new to celebrate; a giggle, a shuffle, a first word, a first step. Brandon was an easy-going, contented little boy who smiled a lot, and I wanted to share our happiness.

In their own way, my parents loved him too. Dad nicknamed him 'Chunk' and Mum enjoyed bouncing him on her knee and making him laugh. They were more attentive as grand-parents than they had been as parents. But always, I felt an undercurrent of resentment and hostility. They didn't approve of my parenting skills any more than I approved of theirs. I didn't let them smoke or take drugs around Brandon and when I visited, I'd throw open the doors and windows for fresh air.

"Smoke is very harmful for babies," I told them.

They'd had eight children of their own, and yet this wasn't something they had considered. Mum rolled her eyes, and Dad jumped in with a nasty comment.

"What, it's good enough for us, but it's not good for you and your baby?" he sneered. "Who do you think you are?"

Another day, I'd bought Brandon a brand-new outfit from Mothercare, complete with his first cute pair of trainers.

"You're so stuck up," Dad said. "Why do you turn up here, showing off?"

I was used to his jibes, yet they stung all the same. I didn't want Brandon's upbringing polluted by unkindness and smoke. Yes, I wanted better for him. I wanted health, happiness, and safety for him. What mother wouldn't? Why was that so wrong? To shield Brandon, I changed my routine and called in on my parents after work, before collecting him from nursery. But they found fault with that too.

"Look at you," Mum said spitefully, nodding towards the skirt and blouse I wore for work. "Honestly, I don't think you're one of mine. You don't fit in here. You think you're better than us."

If it was a joke, then it was a sour one. I was crushed.

I'd devoted my life to my mother, and I adored her. Every time she let me down, I made excuses for her. But now that Brandon was being targeted too, I couldn't just let it go. Perhaps my mother was bitter or envious. Maybe her brain was so drug-addled that she just couldn't think straight. But I couldn't understand it. What mother in their right mind would want a childhood like I'd had? I'd hoped my mother might be proud that I was striving for more for my son. Instead, she was mocking me for it. Emotionally, I was exiled from the family. In spite of all I had done for her – or perhaps because of it – she was casting me out. How dare I want a better life? I was on a different path, and she resented me for it.

The raw truth was that I had survived what she could not. My mother's cruelty struck right to my core, but even then, I could not walk out on her. She needed me. Scratch away at the surface and she was a seven-year-old child; feisty and loud but also vulnerable and afraid. As always, she was my responsibility.

When Brandon was 18 months old, Jude and I separated but remained friends. As a single mum, I was under more pressure and more scrutiny. I saw my status as a reason to work harder, try harder, and be a better parent. I juggled my work with looking after Mum and my siblings and running my own home. But always, my priority was my son. I endured my parents' criticisms, waving away their judgement on Brandon's new coat or his healthy diet, on my promotion at work or my views on drugs. Sadly, I grew to accept they would never be proud of me. Conversely, having relied on me all through my life, they now turned on me like hyenas. I was a punchbag; someone to scoff at and taunt whenever I called round with bags of free shopping. I saw little of Grampy and when I did, I kept Brandon away from him. We bumped into him sometimes down at the shops, but Brandon was either in his buggy or in my arms. Grampy turned up at Mum and Dad's occasionally, but that was always my cue to leave.

I was polite because I had to be. But I was also firm. I never had a conversation with Grampy or spent any time alone with him. There was no opportunity to confront him about the abuse, but neither did I want to. I had spent my life believing I could mend my family, but Grampy could never be fixed. He was beyond repair. In the context of my role as a mother, I glimpsed the enormity of the damage he had done to me, and it was as real as it was raw. I kept the abuse to myself, barricaded away inside my mind; yet another ugly family secret. But I could not eradicate it completely and reminders popped up like boils.

I was plagued by nightmares. I was terrified of intimacy. And that stench was always with me, no matter how often I showered and bathed. I only had to think of Grampy, and of his haunted house, and my skin began to crawl. I took one bath after another, after another. After Brandon turned two, I started to suffer with reoccurring thrush and urine infections. I tried over the counter remedies, but nothing really worked for long. I had abdominal pains too. One night, they became so severe that I ended up in hospital. After a doctor examined me and ran tests, he said, "I haven't encountered this in a long time. Am I right in saying you take a lot of showers or baths?"

I nodded.

"You've washed away your PH balance," he explained. "This is why you're susceptible to thrush and similar conditions. I can prescribe you medication to help in the short term, but I think we need to look at the cause of this."

He had already guessed that my obsession with cleanliness stemmed from childhood sexual abuse, and it was a relief not to have to say it out loud myself. I was sent home with a prescription and a referral for counselling. Soon after, I attended my first appointment.

"So, Tara," said the counsellor. "Where would you like to start?"

As the room filled with silence, I found I could not speak. I felt like my mouth wasn't my own. My memories were entombed so deeply that I could not simply pluck them out on request.

"I'm sorry," I mumbled. "I'm just not ready for this."

I wanted to bury those images deeper than ever, not bring them up for oxygen. I cancelled the counselling. But the abuse remained in the background like a persistent drumbeat.

On a rare night out soon after, I met a new partner, Phil. He was well-built, with dark hair and stunning blue eyes. As we chatted, I learned he came from a close, loving family, and this appealed to me almost as much as Phil did. I wanted stability and warmth for me and Brandon. At the end of 2008, I missed a period. Much as I wanted another baby, I was terrified. I was mid-way through another course of Roaccutane for my skin and had been warned of the dangers of the drug in pregnancy. I booked an urgent appointment with my GP.

"We'd advise you to consider termination," he said. "There are risks to your baby, including miscarriage and severe birth defects."

"No way," I replied. "I'm not having a termination. I can't do it. My baby is here for a reason."

I stopped taking Roaccutane immediately, but each day brought fresh anxiety as I faced the fear that I might lose my baby. The slightest twinge sent me into a frenzy. I had extra antenatal care and scans but if anything, they made me panic even more. I was mistrustful of the doctors and midwives. Each time they recommended something, I questioned if they were secretly trying to terminate my baby. I had been raised not to trust anyone in authority, and it was ingrained in me, like a deep scratch. So when the midwife advised me to increase my dose of folic acid, I at first refused.

"I'm not doing anything to hurt my baby," I told her.

"I'm trying to help your baby," she replied patiently. "I'm on your side."

Incredibly, somehow, I reached 12 weeks, and my baby was

holding on. When a scan showed I was carrying a healthy little girl, I was over the moon.

"You're having a little sister!" I told Brandon.

As with my two previous pregnancies, I ate healthily. I also developed a bizarre craving for soil. I had been out for a walk with Brandon and our dog, Roxy, and as I let myself into the flat, I suddenly scooped a handful of plant pot soil into my mouth. I was in complete shock, and yet at the same time it felt perfectly natural. I was just following my instincts. After that, out with the pram and the dog, I'd find myself eyeing up patches of soil, though I limited myself to eating only my own garden! When I sheepishly confided in the health visitor, she laughed.

"It's not as uncommon as you might think," she told me. "Your body is telling you that you need those nutrients."

Phil and I married the following year at Swindon register Office. It was important that we were a family unit, ready for our new arrival. But my wedding day was not the romantic fairytale occasion I would have liked. I was eight months pregnant by the time our big day came around, and I felt uncomfortable in my plain linen dress, which was too small across my bump. Mum agreed to come but Dad shook his head derisively.

"Weddings are not my thing," he said.

It did not occur to me that he might, according to tradition, have given me away. I just accepted his decision. Really, I had no idea what happened at these formal occasions. My own parents were not married, and I'd never been to a wedding before. Phil's parents helped with the organising and his mum put on a reception back at her house. I felt woefully underprepared as I walked down the aisle, at once too old and too young for all the fuss. Afterwards at the reception, I began to worry that Mum might do something to upset me. Even on my wedding day, my family embarrassed me; Dad, most of all, by his absence. Just four weeks later, I went into labour, and after 12 hours in the hospital, my midwife pressed the panic button.

"Your baby is in distress," she told me. "You need a C-section."

My rush of panic was tempered by the reminder that Brandon had been born healthy after a similar emergency. When I opened my eyes, groggy and exhausted after surgery, a midwife handed me a tiny bundle.

"Here," she beamed. "Meet your daughter."

My heart swelled impossibly with love as I drank in her perfect little face; her eyes like deep blue pools, her cheeks soft and pink. My baby girl, Shania, was born on May 21, 2009, weighing 7lbs 2oz. She was beautiful and perfectly healthy. Phil had a house waiting for us in the Midlands, near where he worked. His job often took him away from home, meaning that it was just me and the children most of the time. I didn't drive, and the house was on the edge of a village. We were very isolated, and yet, I loved it. Brandon started school and I loved the walk, twice a day.

On our way home, we might stop off at the park or call in at the local shop. Like her big brother, Shania was such a happy baby. I only had to peer under the hood of her pram for her to giggle at me and reach out two chubby hands. Brandon was a typical little boy. He was mischievous and giggly and loved trains. He was a big fan of *In the Night Garden*, and especially Iggle Piggle. Seeing my children's characters unfurl was like watching the best film in the world. I was spellbound. I didn't have a single photograph of myself throughout my whole childhood; my parents had never thought to take one.

And so, my own infancy became a blueprint for how not to be with Brandon and Shania. I took photos every day, documenting a grazed knee, a new football, a favourite teddy bear. Each milestone was captured and preserved, framed around my home and in my heart. This was the first time I had been away from my wider family, and it was both alarming and liberating. I worried just the same about Mum and my younger siblings, yet now that I was so far away, there was nothing practical that I could do. I called home every day to check they were okay. But my involvement stopped there. I was absolved from all responsibilities and stress, and it was healing for me and my children to be away from the bitterness. I didn't want my little ones around violence and drugs.

A small part of me hoped my parents might learn to appreciate me, whilst I was gone. But instead, they blamed me for having the nerve to leave them in the first place.

"Was Swindon not good enough for you?" Mum asked,

when I called. "You couldn't wait to get away from us, could you?"

Other times, she would cry and plead with me to go back.

"You just left me," she sobbed. "I can't manage without you, Tar. You know I can't."

Part of me felt compelled to jump on the next train to see her. I was so glad that I had Brandon and Shania to anchor me, and my loyalty lay with them. Not only had they brought me joy as a mother, but they had helped me to leave behind the toxicity of my childhood.

When Shania was 18 months old my marriage ended unexpectedly. I found myself completely alone, with two children and nowhere to live. We moved back to Swindon and, whilst my ex-partners contributed what they could financially, I was short of money, and so we found ourselves in emergency B&B accommodation.

There was a depressing damp smell as we trailed up the stairs to the third floor, where we were allocated one room, with two single beds, a cot and a sink.

The window was broken, and I was petrified of Brandon hurting himself or falling through it. I couldn't take my eyes off him for a second. There was a shared bathroom which I was too afraid to use. I couldn't leave the children on their own and besides, I was worried who I might meet in there.

Each morning, I washed myself and the children at the sink. Each night, I went to bed with a child in each arm.

"Why are we here, Mummy?" Brandon asked. "I don't like it."

"I know," I soothed. "It won't be long. I'll find us a nice new house, I promise."

I was on the council waiting list but because I'd been living out of the area, I was told I might have to wait a while. I applied for a crisis loan but was warned it wouldn't land immediately. I desperately needed a job. Brandon was enrolled at a local school, but Shania was not yet two years old. I'd already applied for a couple of shop jobs, but could only work school hours, so I didn't even get an interview. Besides, I had nobody to look after Shania until a nursery place became available. I couldn't afford to pay a childminder, and anyway, I didn't want to leave my children with a stranger. Another hangover from the abuse was that I was suspicious of everyone and I was overprotective of Brandon and Shania.

One afternoon, we went out for a walk and Brandon started to complain he was hungry. At the cashpoint, I punched my pin in to check my balance and my knees almost buckled in despair. £1.30 credit. I bought a sandwich for the children to share, ignoring my own rumbling stomach. I was destitute. Back at the hostel I lay in bed wide awake with sheer stress, whilst the children slept either side of me. This could not carry on. But what could I do? I needed money quickly. Tears slid down my cheeks and onto Shania, who was snuggled into my neck. I had reached yet another soul-crushing nadir.

Yet as was always the way, I recognised that the only path forward was a positive one. And by the time morning came, I had an idea.

Back when Brandon was a baby, I'd become friendly with a neighbour who worked as a stripper in a club in Swindon.

"I could never do that," I gasped.

"Oh, you'd be surprised," she replied. "I used to think that. But now I earn a fortune. I can't imagine ever giving it up."

I didn't want to offend her, but it really wasn't for me. Yet as weak, grey, daylight seeped in through the thin hostel curtains, I realised I no longer had a choice. This was my only way out of here. I still had her number, and, after the school run, I gave her a call.

"Sure," she said. "I'll send you the details of the club. Give them my name when you call."

I set up an interview and quickly found a childminder, recommended by a couple of friends. Now that I was paying for childcare, I was under pressure to see this through. But as I tapped timidly on the side door of the club, I thought I was going to be sick. And the audition was every bit as excruciating as I had feared.

"And the bra!" shouted the manager, as I stripped down to my underwear in front of him. "Take off the bra!"

Inwardly, I was cringing, crying with embarrassment. Already, I deeply regretted getting myself into this. I resolved to agree with whatever he said and then forget the audition had ever happened.

"Okay, you can have a shift on Saturday," he told me. "You'll make £750 a night with tips."

The figures spun round in my head like reels on a slot-machine. Ker-ching! I couldn't believe it. With that kind of money, we could be out of the hostel and into our own place within weeks.

"Yes," I replied. "I'll be here."

Yet as I waited for the weekend to come, I oscillated back and forth. The money was too good to turn down, and one night's wage was more than I'd earn in a month at any other part-time job. And yet, I wasn't sure I could do it. Growing up, I'd felt like a piece of meat, something to be ogled, passed around, used and abused. I thought of Grampy, of the perverted police officer, of all the predators I'd met at Sammy's house. I'd worked so hard to put all that behind me, to build a new life for myself and my children. So why was I willingly putting myself under a predatory spotlight again?

"You're doing it for Brandon and Shania," I reminded myself.

Yet what if they found out what I was doing? What if I was recognised at the club, and word got out? I imagined a horrendous scene at the school gates, a confrontation with supercilious mothers who no longer wanted their son or daughter to play with Brandon because of his mother's wayward morals.

"So, you're a stripper! You take your clothes off for men? My god, I'm disgusted."

I could not take that risk. I could not allow my own children to be subjected to the same shame and bullying as I had as a child. I could not do to them what had been done to me. And yet neither could I leave them living in a hostel where they were neither happy nor safe. *£750 a night*. The figures spoke for themselves. The arguments ran back and forth in my mind during another sleepless night. The next morning, Shania cut her finger on a nail sticking out of the banister, and she burst into tears. It was the final push I needed.

"We're moving out of here soon," I promised them. "After school later, we'll make a chart and tick off the days."

There was no going back. I could not let my children down. But that first night, I was flushed with nerves and apprehension. Waiting in line, I was trembling so much that I half-feared and half-hoped the manager might sack me on the spot. Stepping out onto the stage, I was thrust back suddenly, to the age of 10, with strangers leering as I ran through the house in my Minnie Mouse nightie.

"Tomorrow will come," I told myself softly. "This will pass."

Somehow, I got through it. I closed my eyes, ignoring the cheers and the whistles, and pretended I was flying outside with the birds, just as I had when I was small. On my break, I hurried to the toilets and locked myself in. Again, I was a child, hiding in the toilet block at school, a million worries hurtling through my mind.

"Tomorrow is coming," I whispered.

Soon, I had a regular slot at the club. My stage name was Faith, and I worked Friday, Saturday and Sunday nights, 12-4am. I was forever getting into trouble for not taking my bra off quickly on stage or not smiling enough. And as soon as my time was done, I'd rush to the toilets. The other girls chatted happily over a drink and a cigarette in between performances. But I sat on the loo, on my own, with my head in my hands.

"This will not last," I reminded myself.

One night, two men came into the club, and called me over. My fixed smile faltered as I worried what they were about to ask of me.

"Please relax. We don't want anything from you," said one. "We noticed you don't look comfortable. We just wanted to say hello. You can sit here and talk to us if you like."

I didn't know whether to be pleased or disgusted. They were trying to help, and yet they were customers in a strip club. I didn't want their support and certainly not their pity. My view of relationships, already twisted out of shape by the abuse, was further contorted by the men I danced for. Many, doubtless, had wives, girlfriends, mothers, sisters and daughters at home. How many of them would ever admit they paid women to strip? And yet who was I to judge? I was the one making it all possible. I felt so ashamed, so complicit. I had to be honest with the childminder, to explain my odd hours, but she just smiled.

"You do what you have to do," she told me. "Your children are safe here with me."

In-between working and looking after the children, I was still popping home every day to check on Mum and my siblings.

"You look shattered," Mum told me one morning. "And you've got last night's make-up on. Was it a good night then?"

I shook my head wearily.

"Nothing like that," I sighed. "If you must know, I'm working as a stripper. I need to get the kids out of the hostel, and the money is good."

I don't know what reaction I expected, but Mum threw her arms around me and whooped.

"That's amazing!" she exclaimed. "Well! My girl is a stripper. I am so proud of you, Tar."

I was speechless. All my life, I had tried to make Mum proud. As a child myself, helping out with the little ones, I hoped she'd notice. I thought she might praise me when I did a school run, or I made beans on toast, or I went to a parents' evening on her behalf. But she never did. I expected she might be proud when I became a mother. Or when I got my first job. When I got a better job. When I got my own home. When I got married. But no. She had no opinion about any of those milestones. But now that I was a stripper, I had finally made her proud.

Soaked through with sadness and confusion, I turned away to hide my pain. I thought of Shania, so pure and innocent at two years old. It would break me in half if she was forced to turn to stripping to make ends meet. Yet my own mother was thrilled. I don't judge women who strip professionally. If it works for you then that's great. But it absolutely didn't work for me.

As a survivor of trauma, I saw all men as predators and I saw all sex as abuse. Stripping night after night caused me to relive the attacks, over and over and over. Each time I slipped off my gown ready to dance, I rewound back to childhood. I was at the top of the stairs in my Minnie Mouse nightie. I was in the bath at Grampy's, waiting for the birds to rescue me. I was in the spare room, with that smell stinging my nostrils.

"Remember, take off the bra," my manager reminded me, as I walked past him onto the stage.

"How could I forget?" I muttered.

Seven weeks later, I had saved a deposit and the first month's rent on a nice two bedroomed flat. I handed in my notice at the club, the same day I picked up the keys. And I couldn't deny that I was proud of myself as we walked out of the hostel for the last time.

"Look what you did," I said to myself.

'But look how you did it,' whispered an ugly voice in my head.

I would always have that mental backlash; I was so used to others bringing me down that I automatically did it to myself, though I didn't deserve it. We settled into our new place, and the kids loved it. It was clean and safe, and it was home. First and foremost, as a mother, I did what was best for my children and if I could turn back time, I would do the same thing over again.

14

SOON AFTER Shania turned three, the lease was up on our flat. I decided to look for a house so the children could have a bedroom each and a garden. At short notice, I was offered a viewing on a perfect property. But it was late afternoon, school and nursery had finished, and my childminder wasn't available. I didn't want to lose the house, but I couldn't think of anyone to look after the children right now. Yet even as I called Dad, I couldn't deny I had misgivings.

"Would you be able to look after the children please, just for half an hour?" I asked him. "I have a house viewing. I won't be long I promise."

Dad agreed immediately.

"Please don't smoke around them," I asked him, as I dropped them off. "I'll be as quick as I can."

I rushed through the viewing, and, when I arrived to pick up the children, Dad answered the door with a cigarette dangling from his mouth. Brandon and Shania were either side of him and Mum was in the background.

"Dad!" I exclaimed. "I asked you not to smoke!"

His lip curled and I instantly regretted opening my mouth.

"Don't tell me what I can and can't do," he snarled. "Always the same with you, Tara. Bossing everyone about, thinking you're better than the rest of us. If I want to smoke, I will smoke."

I didn't reply. He followed me into the house and, as I quickly gathered the kids' things, I felt Dad's breath on the back of my neck. With a sharp shove from behind, my head hit the computer table hard, and my nose exploded. There was blood everywhere. Brandon was crying and Shania was screaming. Somehow, I strapped her into her buggy and grabbed Brandon's hand. My face was covered in blood, it was all over my clothes and my hands and already, my head was throbbing with pain. As we reached the door, Mum lunged at me, pulling me back by my hair. I fell to the ground, almost pulling the buggy over with me. She stood over me, her face twisted with anger.

"Who do you think you are?" she hissed.

The police arrived moments later alerted, no doubt, by neighbours who had heard the screaming. But even as I was helped away by an officer, Mum had to be held back. She was like a wild cat, desperate to sink her claws into me.

"Who are these people?" asked the officer. "Do you know them?"

The answer pained me far more than my injuries.

"They're my parents," I mumbled, spitting blood. "My mum and dad."

In hospital, my eyebrow was glued. I had cuts and bruises too. But the mental scars, I knew, would take far longer to heal. I was numb with shock. How could my own mother attack me like that? I could not reconcile this with the woman I adored. Had I been lying to myself, all these years? I'd had beatings like that from Dad in the past, but never in front of my children. Brandon and Shania had never seen violence like that, and it took them days to settle down afterwards. I was furious my parents had put them through that.

Mum was arrested and cautioned but I could not face pressing charges against her. I lost my part-time job in a shop because of my facial injuries, and I lost the tenancy on the house too.

With no money, we found ourselves once again reliant on the authorities which was so frustrating. I was advised to stay in a women's refuge, at least until my parents calmed down. Appalled, I didn't see why I should be the one to be punished. And yet, I didn't want to face them in court. I couldn't see another solution.

The refuge was on the other side of town so would at least put some distance between us. We were given a double room with a telly balanced on a chest of drawers. It was cleaner than the B&B and, because it was exclusively women and children, I didn't feel unsafe. But Brandon was perplexed by the behaviour of the other kids.

"Why won't they play with me?" he asked. "Why aren't they friendly?"

I remembered myself at that age, and I knew why they were folded inwards, like little flowers at night. The world was not kind to them and so they shied away.

"They're probably very sad," I said to Brandon.

I didn't want my children in this environment, I felt like I was slipping back into my own childhood. The women had stories of hardship, they had been stalked, harassed, beaten, by ex-boyfriends and ex-husbands.

"What about you?" they asked.

"I'm here because of my parents," I muttered, scalded by a shame that was not even mine.

I was the only woman in there who needed protection from her own mother. How could that be? As with the abuse, I began to question myself. Was this my fault? Had I somehow triggered the attack? Every time I tried to move on with my life, my parents did their best to drag me back down. Why? Did they hate me, as I had feared when I was small? Three weeks on, we were given a council house in a new area. But despite the physical distance between me and my parents, the contact continued. I no longer took Brandon and Shania there with me, but I visited most days, taking bags of food, doing cleaning and laundry. Cameron was still at primary school, and I wanted to keep an eye on him. Even now, I could not cut my mother adrift. She needed me and, in my own way, I needed her too. For their part, my parents behaved as though nothing had happened. For them, the attack was just another minor drama. It was no big deal.

Later that year, I enrolled at college to study social work. Despite my mistrust of the authorities, I appreciated how important they were – or could be – if they did their jobs well. I planned to help lost children like me. Shania started school and she and Brandon were in a strict routine. In contrast to the roller coaster lifestyle of my parents, our lives were ordered, settled and smooth. In time, I hoped they might forget the attack by my parents, though I would never leave my children in their care again. We were just settling back into normality when I got a call from social services, asking if I could look after a relative's baby daughter who had been taken into care.

"You're the only family member we can think of," the social worker said. "Can you help? It will hopefully only be temporary."

Really, I was busy enough looking after my own children. But I couldn't say no. When my family needed me, I had to be there for them. Over the next few weeks, I attended meetings and assessments, before welcoming the little girl into our home. The placement took up so much of my time that I had to give up my college course.

Again, just as I was making progress, I was hauled backwards. Like climbing a mountain, I'd get almost to the summit before someone pushed me back to the bottom. By looking after one family, I was neglecting another – my own. By the time the foster placement came to an end, I had given up on the idea of returning to education. Instead, in 2014,

I got a job at Wallis, a high street fashion brand in the town centre.

By now, Shania was five years old, and Brandon was nearly nine. I loved my new role and was quickly promoted to working in Debenhams as an assistant manager. It was a full-time job, and, like any working single parent, I had to make sacrifices. I did the morning school run, but the child-minder picked the children up in the afternoon. I missed assemblies and school plays and football tournaments. I hated not being there, but my main priority was to provide for my children and give them security. And we treasured the time we had together in the evenings and at weekends. We had more money for days out and treats. With memories of my own miserable childhood still fresh in my mind, I made sure Brandon and Shania wanted for nothing. Collecting coupons from the newspaper, I even saved enough for us to go on our first ever family holiday to Devon.

We stayed in a chalet by the sea, just the three of us, and we had the time of our lives. Together, we built sandcastles, ate picnics, and paddled in the waves. I loved seeing their eyes light up when the ice cream van trundled onto the promenade. I laughed as they ran away from the crabs we found in the rock pools. What they didn't realise was that this was my first ever holiday too. Feeling the sand in my toes and fishing for minnows with a £1 net, I felt like more of a child than I ever had when I was growing up. Returning home to school and work was not the disappointment I had envisaged, because I was filled with motivation to save for our next break. Mum and Dad had been rehoused by the council in the town centre, so I was able to pop in and check on them during my lunch hour from work. One day, I found them in the middle of a furious row. Mum was on the floor, crying.

"He threw a cup of coffee over me," she wailed. "My arms are burning."

I got her to the sink to run cold water over her burns. But Dad was still angry and when I stepped in between them both, he went for me instead. As he grabbed at my hair I had one eye on my watch; I needed to be back at work soon.

"Please, just stop this," I gasped eventually, pushing him away.

I managed to calm them both down before hurrying back to work, smoothing my uniform and retying my ponytail in the staff toilets. Minutes later, I was offering advice to a customer on a wedding outfit. It was a dizzying contrast but, just as when I was small, I was accustomed to playing a role and acting out a part. I hardly knew who I was any more. My persona at work was little more than a façade, with my real life, like my secrets, tucked well away. Soon after, I was leading a team briefing in the office at work when we heard a commotion downstairs.

"Shoplifters," a colleague told me. "A crowd of them and they've turned nasty from the sounds of it."

I tutted at the distant screaming and shouting as I hurried to the escalators. And then, suddenly, my blood froze.

"Get off me! Get off me!" yelled a woman.

I would have recognised that voice anywhere at all. My own mother. I was stunned. She knew, as did my whole family, that I worked at Debenhams. Had they deliberately targeted me here? Why on earth would they do that? As I arrived at the scene, I recognised more family members, brawling with security guards. My mother was in the middle of it all.

"Tar!" she screeched. "Tar!"

I wanted to curl up and disappear. I looked at the floor, wishing it would swallow me, conscious my manager's glare was drilling through the back of my head. I had worked so hard for this, sacrificing time with my children, missing out on milestone events. And in one selfish, thoughtless act, my family had decimated everything. Again. I handed in my notice at work that same day. I could not recover from this. I got the bus home, sick to the pit of my stomach with a shame that my own family had put there. That night, I made a decision. It was time for a new start.

Whilst I was working out my notice at Debenhams, I terminated our rental agreement. On my next day off, after dropping the children at school, I went to the train station and bought a ticket to the end of the line, which happened to be Swansea. And that was the scrutiny with which I picked our new home; I simply chose the last stop on the line because I needed to get as far away as I could from the toxicity in Swindon. I had never been to Swansea before, and I knew nobody there. Almost as if I was being guided by a guardian angel, I got onto the train and spent the day in Swansea looking for a new home, a new job, and new schools for the children. Arriving home that evening, I made an announcement.

"We're moving to Wales!" I told Brandon and Shania.

Behind my bravado, I was terrified but resolute. I spent the week packing and making plans. It was hard saying goodbye to Jasmine because she and I were so close. It broke my heart to be apart from Cameron too; he was my youngest sibling. But I also knew I could no longer stay. Enough was enough. For years, I had tried to stitch together the disparate scraps of our family life.

Now I was walking away, shedding the remnants which had clung like cobwebs to me. I could not save Mum and instead I had to focus on saving my children. This was the time to look after the next generation. It was both liberating and profoundly sad. In between packing boxes, I went to visit Mum, who had, out of the blue, moved in with a new partner. She and Dad were on and off as they always had been. Arriving at an unfamiliar house, I found her unconscious in a bedroom. Gazing at her sleeping face, still so child-like, I was suddenly seized with panic. What if this was the last time I ever saw her? She could so easily overdose and die. Was I doing the right thing by leaving her? Conflicted, I went back to see her a second time, later that week.

This time, she was awake, and we had a photo taken on the sofa together. I tried to tell her that we were leaving but, as with so many other confidences in the past, the words jammed in my throat. Deep down, I knew she'd talk me out of it. I knew she'd cry and wail and plead with me to stay. And I could not take that risk. Instead, at the doorway, I hugged her and said, "Look after yourself, Mum, I love you. I will always love you."

Her smile simultaneously melted my heart and shattered it. I cherished her and I didn't ever want to lose her. But I had to admit I'd been losing her, bit by bit, all of my life. Much as I would miss my family, I could no longer allow for me and my children to keep sinking back under their control. I wanted Brandon and Shania to tread their own path.

Being a good mother was not about pouring my children into a mould which my family approved of. They deserved to be their own person, to find their own colour, shape and size. And I wanted better for them than I had. I dreamed of giving them the moon and the stars. More than anything, I longed for them to have a normal childhood. I wanted them to be safe, happy and loved. Yet if we stayed in Swindon, none of this would be possible.

My family blamed me and made me feel guilty for that, just as they had all my life. And so, to ensure my plan was carried out, we had to leave in secret. I resented letting yet more secrecy into our lives, but I told myself this would be the last one. The following Sunday, we arrived at the station, carrying three suitcases. I had booked a van to follow on with the rest of our possessions. Settling into my seat on the train, I took in a deep breath, right to the bottom of my lungs. As we shunted slowly out of the station, I said, as much to myself as to the children, "We're going to have such an amazing life."

As we picked up pace, they bounced up and down in excitement and I stared out of the window. The towns and fields whizzing past soon became a kaleidoscope of scenes from my old life. In each image I saw Mum, Dad and Grampy. I remembered the police raids, the fights with Dad, the endless worries over Mum. I was catapulted back to the night of Jasmine's overdose as a toddler. I rewound back to my visits to Sammy's and shuddered as I recognised the creeps who had groomed me. I brushed away a tear as I pictured Hammy, stiff and cold in his cage. Another flash, and there I was, hiding in the school toilets, worrying whether I might be pregnant at the age of nine. As I watched my chequered childhood shrinking in the rear-view mirror, the fingertips of the past were slowly peeled back one by one, and Swindon loosened its grip on me at last.

The hissing and screeching noise of the train was the sound of my past being obliterated. And ahead, lay freedom and hope. I smiled as Brandon and Shania sounded out the names of the stations as we passed through. This was a journey filled with possibilities; our physical relocation mirrored by emotional upheaval. That picture of us on the train became a perfectly framed postcard in my mind. I wanted to press pause and make it last forever, because none of us really knew what lay ahead.

15

I HAD rented a two bedroomed house, with a nice long back garden, and a spacious kitchen diner. We were exhausted by the time we arrived, but the kids were easily distracted, unpacking their toys and teddies, running around the garden, and jumping on the new beds. I was braced for a challenge.

With debts mounting from our move, I began working two jobs the following week. I got a full-time role in the medical records department in the local hospital, and a part-time evening job at a call centre. I found a childminder for the children, and they started at a new primary school. But those fledgling steps were not easy.

Brandon, in particular, had good friends back in Swindon and had been upset to leave them all behind. When the initial gloss of our adventure faded, he became homesick and wanted to see his old pals again. He didn't settle in well in his new class.

Shania was uncharacteristically quiet too. Normally, she was a real tomboy, she loved playing football and racing around with Brandon and his mates. But she became clingy and shy each morning at the school gates. They were both struggling to adjust.

"It will get easier," I reassured them. "I promise."

Some nights though, with my feet throbbing after a double shift at work, I questioned myself. I knew nobody here. I was so alone, and so isolated. Had I been foolish to think I could simply trampoline my way to eternal bliss, just by bouncing into a new town and a new life.

Truth was, I was not even aiming for happiness. Peace and normality would have done me just fine. But these were alien concepts to me, and I was unsure if I would find them in Swansea. I worried that perhaps I was the problem, not my parents, not Swindon, not Swansea. But me. I remembered the way Dad had screwed up his face as he snarled:

"You're nothing, Tara! You think you're better than me but you're nothing!"

What if he was right all along?

"No, I told myself firmly. "Give it time. Tomorrow will come. Tomorrow is a better day."

And little by little, as the weeks passed, my mantra stood firm, and we began to carve out a new life. We made new friends through school and work. The childminder became one of my best friends and I got to know our neighbours. And though I was busy, working two jobs and raising two children, I thrived on the urgency and the pressure. I welcomed that sense of purpose and the ability to provide for my family and I was soothed and anchored by the simplicity and predictability of our routine.

"I like it here, Mum," Brandon told me after a school football match. "I don't ever want to go back to Swindon."

One winters morning in January 2015, I was walking the children to school when we were caught in a violent hailstorm. It was miserable, trudging up the big hill near our home with bullets of ice stinging our cold faces. One particularly powerful gust of wind lifted Shania off her feet, and she fell backwards to the ground.

Quickly I scooped her up and tried to dry her tears. But by the time we arrived at the school gates, we were all soaked through. On my walk home, I cried too. I hated to think of my children squelching around school all day in wet socks and shoes. I reminded myself there would be lots of children with wet socks that day, but that just made me cry even more. I seemed to feel each hardship so keenly, worse than if it was my own. I could not shake the feeling that I was letting my children down. Because my own childhood had been so miserable, I wanted theirs to be perfect and so I was striving, always, for something which did not exist. After work that night, I told them, "I'm going to learn to drive, then we don't need to walk to school in the rain ever again."

It was an ambitious statement, but once I had made my promise, I could not backtrack. I booked driving lessons that same week and a couple of months later, I was the proud owner of a small white Hyundai. Shania could not wait for another hailstorm, so that we could arrive in school in style! It was so important to me that I never let my children down.

My childhood had been littered with broken promises and false starts, and I understood only too well how painful that was. So many times, I'd turned up at school without a coat or a gym kit or a pencil case. That feeling of worthlessness, which came from being abused, was reinforced every time I was singled out for not being the same as all the other children. I resolved that Brandon and Shania would never feel that shame.

At birthdays and Christmas, I made sure they had everything they dreamed of and more, with parties, cakes and gifts. I was, probably, over-attentive and over-indulgent. But way beyond the material extravagance, most important of all, was that they were loved. And nobody was more loved than they were.

Since moving to Swansea, I'd completely severed contact with Grampy. Any meetings we'd had in recent years had been accidental, at the shops or at my parents' house. Here in Swansea, I would never bump into him again. The relief that my children were safe from him was worth all the teething problems from our move.

Despite that final showdown in Debenhams, I kept in touch with Mum. It was inexplicable, even to myself, that no matter what she did, I forgave her. My love for her was unconditional, like a mother with a child. As I'd predicted, she reacted badly when she found out we'd left the country.

"You think you're too good to live in Swindon, like us, don't you?" she said.

I tried explaining that it was nothing to do with her and that I needed a fresh start. But she took it as a personal insult that I had my own house, car and career. What was commonplace for other families was unthinkable in mine. I was an outcast purely because I had learned to drive and I worked. Paradoxically, I was both a conformist and a rebel, depending on whether I was judged by society or my family.

"I don't know why you've turned out like that," Mum scoffed.

She was behaving as though I had ruined my life. Yet by coming to Swansea, I had surely saved it. I knew by now I had to fireproof my heart against her criticism. Some days, she didn't pick up the phone to me. Other times, her number might be switched off or disconnected. Late at night, I'd find myself calling everyone we knew, asking them to check on her.

Again, she was like a child to me; I was the frantic parent, ringing round when a teenager failed to come home after a night out. Even aged 49, Mum was as wayward and irresponsible as ever. And so, though I was far away, I worried just as much. Despite her sniping and her moaning, our circuit remained intact.

The thread which bound us had slackened and frayed, but it never snapped. I had been in Swansea only three months when Swindon social services got in touch and asked if

Cameron could come to stay with me. He had been taken into care, away from my parents, and I was, they said, his only option. I felt a jab of guilt as the social worker spoke. I had not been there as much for Cameron when he was growing up, because he was so much younger than the others.

By the time he was born, I was almost ready to leave home myself. Was this why he had been taken into care, because I was not there for him? I had let him down, and the shame cut through my throat like a shard of glass. Social services could and should, in my opinion, have stepped in on many occasions when me and my siblings were growing up. But poor Cameron was the only one they had taken away. I felt I owed him.

"Of course," I agreed. "He can come here."

Besides, he and I were intrinsically linked from his birth. I had helped to deliver him and that bond was still there despite the physical chasm between us. I could never have turned him away. We were well settled in Swansea, and the children and I were flourishing, in part thanks to the distance between us and my parents. I thought a new start would do Cameron good too. It would be difficult, certainly. But we would manage somehow. I could not bear the thought of him all alone in a children's home. But no sooner had I given consent to the social worker, than Mum called.

"You're not happy with taking my grandchildren away from me, now you want Cameron as well?" she yelled. "You've betrayed me."

"Mum, that's not how it is," I replied.

Cameron was already in social services care; I was offering him a home, not taking one away. But Mum did not see that, or at least she did not want to see it. Instead of thanking me, she blamed me. It was a pattern she had followed all my life, and I was weary of it. Yet still, I made excuses for her. I reminded myself she was fragile and vulnerable, and she was lashing out at me only because she was afraid. Whilst I was undergoing the necessary checks and assessments to foster Cameron, I tried to keep in touch with her every day. I wanted us to be on friendly terms, for Cameron's sake too. One afternoon, she said to me:

"Kylie is having some trouble from two sisters on her estate."

Kylie was my younger sister and Mum said she was being targeted by two sisters named Charice and Amberstasia Gassman. Automatically, my hackles went up. Even in Swansea, I was still the mother hen. I wanted to look after her.

"Is it a problem?" I asked. "I can help."

Mum laughed.

"No, I can deal with it," she replied. "They're picking on Kylie because they're bullies, that's all they are. I can keep an eye on her."

Whilst Mum needed protection in some ways, she was, conversely, more than capable of defending herself or her children in an argument. I had been on the receiving end of her temper only recently and I could vouch for that. Even so, I made sure to call Kylie to check on her. She told me the Gassmans had initially befriended her and visited her flat. But then they turned. When Kylie went to the shops, they started calling her names.

"Have they been violent?" I asked. "Have they threatened you?"

"No," Kylie replied. "Nothing like that. Just name-calling."

We were all in agreement that the Gassmans were a neighbourhood nuisance and nothing more.

16

BY APRIL 2015, we had been in Swansea for five months and were happier than we'd ever been. Our days were busy, juggling school and work, birthday parties and football tournaments, sleepovers and homework projects. I was also preparing for Cameron to move in as soon as social services had completed the assessments.

For the first time, my life was beginning to look and feel almost normal. Growing up, the lack of routine and predictability at home had panicked me. I was unsafe and untethered. Here, in my own little house, many miles from the predator who had ruined my innocence, I welcomed the sense of order. It was so comforting to feel secure and anchored. But one night, I was washing dishes at the sink when, without warning, I had a brutal flashback to my childhood. Closing my eyes, I saw the red toy bus and the yellow teapot in the cupboard under the stairs. I heard Grampy grunting. I could smell him so pungently, he might as well have been right next to me.

"No!" I shuddered, opening my eyes. "Leave me alone!"

I shook my head to dislodge the recollection. I didn't want this. Why now? But later that night, I was assaulted by another memory. Then another. They were like vultures, swooping down on me to pick over the carcass of my childhood. Some scenes had been buried so deeply that I had forgotten them completely – until now. My brain began releasing snippets of horror on a drip feed. Each ossified memory was a splinter right through my core. The pain quite literally took my breath away.

Gathering my strength, I tried to reel in the memories and examine them. Some were painfully, horrifyingly, clear. Some were distorted and fragmented, like reflections in water. And others, like the toys under the stairs, like the attack in the spare room, were too far out at sea. I could not reach them, and I wasn't sure I wanted to. Like pages ripped from a book, my recollections were incomplete. I didn't understand why, now I was happy and settled, I was being ambushed by spectres from my past. Why wouldn't they let me move on as I wished? I wasn't sleeping or eating properly, and I was distracted at work. Eventually, I made an appointment with my GP.

"Bad things happened to me as a child," I told her. "Now that I'm getting my life in order, the memories are all resurfacing. I don't understand it."

"It's precisely because you're settled that your subconscious is releasing these memories," she told me. "You're in a good place. You can cope with it. That's why you're getting these reminders."

She was so kind and patient that I found myself confiding in her a little of what had happened with Grampy.

"I'm getting physical pains in my pelvis as well," I told her. "It's almost like the abuse is happening all over again."

"That's perfectly normal too," she told me. "This pain was held in your memory. You could not allow yourself to hurt at the time, so you are hurting now. It will be helpful for you to bring these memories into the open. You can't bury them forever. Let me know when you feel ready to see a counsellor and I can help you."

I left the appointment in tears of gratitude. I had learned so much, in one single consultation. I was beginning to understand that the layers under which I had hidden the abuse had been protective but also smothering. Burying the abuse had also meant burying a part of myself, and I knew my GP was right. Talking about this, dredging up those deeply interred memories, could only be a positive decision. But I was not sure I was ready yet. Each time I thought of the red bus and the yellow teapot, my heart galloped with fear and I told myself not knowing the truth might be easier after all. Instead, I stayed busy constantly. Even after the kids were in bed, and it was my chance to sit down and relax, I was on the go. I cleaned until midnight, sometimes even later. As I polished and scrubbed, I realised that, like Mum, I was trying to wash away the stains of the past.

It was one evening around the beginning of May 2015 when Mum answered the phone in tears.

"What's the matter?" I asked.

"I'm sorry, I'm sorry, I'm not good enough," she sobbed.

"Mum, that's not true," I told her. "You will always be good enough for me."

"I'm not a good mother, I've lost Cameron," she wept. "I miss him so much."

"You haven't lost him," I insisted. "I don't want to take him away from you. I want to help. He will be able to come home if you do what the social workers tell you."

She seemed to calm down a little. She told me she was drinking heavily but, in the hope that Cameron might be allowed home, she said she had been clean from drugs for several weeks. I didn't believe her, but I kept my doubts to myself.

"Well done," I said. "I'm proud of you."

By the time our call ended, she sounded a bit brighter. She was certainly more lucid and reasonable than she had been for a while.

"I love you," I told her, as we said goodbye.

Twelve days later, on a Tuesday afternoon, I was at work in the call centre when I took a call from an elderly man who explained his wife had died leaving him all alone. He became upset and tearful, and I felt tears running down my own cheeks as I listened. I felt so sorry for him. After the call ended, I sank my head into my hands and took a deep breath. I was a little dizzy and disorientated.

"You've had too much coffee," one of my colleagues said. "Have a glass of water."

"You're right," I nodded.

But I couldn't stop thinking about the old man, lonely in his grief, forgotten by the rest of the world. As I was leaving work later, I spotted a Facebook update about a fatal stabbing in Swindon near to where Kylie lived. There were no more details, and I swiped onto my playlist so that I could listen to music on the bus. Next stop was the childminder, where I collected the children.

"Are you okay, Tara?" she asked. "You look a bit peaky."

"I'm fine," I smiled. "Just a stressful shift at work."

But even as we walked home, and I tuned in to the kids chattering away, I still felt a little off. I wondered if I was coming down with something. As I turned the key in the door, I spotted a missed call from Jasmine, and I rang her back as the kids were dumping their schoolbags and coats and running into the kitchen for snacks. Jasmine answered the phone immediately, screaming like I had never heard her scream before.

"What's happened? What's wrong?" I gasped.

Jasmine was still screaming, unable to get her breath or to speak. I thought she was having a panic attack.

"Breathe," I said. "Breathe with me. Deep breath, come on, Jazzy."

She gulped sharply and then she whispered: "She's gone."

"Who?" I asked, but even as I spoke, I knew. I just knew. A curl of fear wrapped itself around my heart, squeezing tighter and tighter until my breath was coming in short and painful gasps.

"Mum," Jasmine choked. "Mum's dead."

"Did she overdose?" I asked, sinking to the floor in the hallway as the words left my mouth. It felt like a betrayal, saying them out loud, as though I was making it true. I'd dreaded this moment for as long as I could remember. Since I was a small child, I had lived under the constant threat that the drugs would kill my mother in the end. And now, my prophecy had self-fulfilled.

"Drugs," I muttered to myself.

But Jasmine said, "Mum was murdered. She was stabbed this afternoon, Tara. The Gassman sisters attacked her in the street outside Kylie's flat."

Shock burned through me like a clean white flame. I tried to speak, to protest, but I felt like someone was pouring sand down my throat. I couldn't breathe. The world seemed to stutter to a halt as I lay slumped on the carpet. I had no idea where I was or how long I'd been there, when a loud banging at the door sliced through my stupor.

"Police!" shouted a voice.

There was no strength in my legs. I crawled on my hands and knees to the front door, still wearing my coat and boots from work. My lanyard swung from my neck, like a cruel reminder of an old life. There was no going back now. And no going forwards either.

"Your neighbour heard you crying and called us," an officer explained. "What's wrong?"

Through my sobs, I explained my mother had been killed.

“Have you not had any contact from the police in Swindon?” they asked.

I shook my head numbly. The officers made sure I was okay and arranged for my neighbour to come and look after the children. After they were tucked up in bed asleep, she went home.

“If you need me, I’m just next door,” she said kindly.

The day had seemed long, but the night was endless. Time folded in on itself, slipped backwards, and seemed to slow to a halt. And as reality hit me, in those lonely hours when it was darkest, my grief coagulated into anger. I was furious the police had not informed me of Mum’s death before it was posted on social media. There was even CCTV of her murder circulating online. In a rush, I realised I hadn’t asked Jasmine how on earth it had happened, and whether the attackers had been arrested. Though it was 3am, I knew she’d be awake.

“Yes,” she told me. “The Gassman sisters have been arrested. Remember they were harassing Kylie? There was a row in the shop, Mum stood up to Charice so she followed her back to Kylie’s and stabbed her.”

I reeled, each word like a sledgehammer at the back of my head. The Gassman sisters, who we had all dismissed as harmless bullies, had ambushed Mum, attacked her in the street outside Kylie’s flat, and left her to die in a pool of her own blood.

“I was studying in the library when I heard there’d been a

stabbing outside Kylie's block," Jasmine told me. "I ran all the way there, but there was a police cordon. I was begging them to let me see Mum, but they wouldn't let me through."

I felt helpless, being so far away. I wanted to take Jasmine in my arms and dry her tears, just as I had when she was a toddler. I blamed myself, believing if I hadn't moved away, Mum would still be alive. Irrationally, I convinced myself I could somehow have saved her, I could have stepped in to protect her or even prevented the attack before it began. I was her mother figure, and I had let her down. Unforgivably, I had abandoned her when she needed me most. Over and over, staring at my phone in the darkness, I watched the CCTV footage from the attack.

It tore me apart, yet it was like a punishment, a form of self-harm, and I forced myself to keep playing it. It ended each time with Mum lying on the ground; a tiny, defenceless figure, in a crumpled heap. She looked like a child, and in many ways, she was. I imagined myself climbing into the scene and somehow changing the ending, running towards her, and fighting off her attackers. I kept on pressing play, as though this time, the ending might be different, and Mum might still be alive. Each time I saw her on the ground, my heart cracked all over again.

"Mum, get up," I pleaded. "Get up off the floor!"

My mind swirled with confusion. In one moment, I was brimming with superhuman anger and energy as though I had the strength to sprint back to Swindon, to turn back time and to save my mother. In the next minute, I was drained and defeated and utterly bereft. I could not move forward without her. And yet at the same time, I questioned whether it was all true. The distance allowed me to lie to myself and to cast doubt on the facts. Perhaps it wasn't Mum in the CCTV clip. Maybe everyone had made a mistake. There was a good chance she was curled up on her mattress at home in Swindon. I did not sleep at all and the next morning, as soon as the children were awake, we set off up the M4. Jasmine was waiting as we turned into the road where she now lived.

"Are you sure it's Mum?" I asked her. "Could there be a mix-up?"

In the cold and unforgiving light of day, I realised how hopeless that sounded.

"I saw her, Tara," she replied sadly. "I saw her on the floor. It took ages for the paramedics to move her. It was horrible."

Poor Jasmine was traumatised and again, I blamed myself. I'd looked after my little sister all my life; why wasn't I here at the moment she most needed me? That same afternoon, I saw Kylie. She had witnessed it all.

"The Gassman sisters threw a bike against my door and started causing trouble, so I called Mum," Kylie told me. "She got the bus over and we met up in the local shop."

But Charice Gassman was also in the shop, and she had started a row. Outwardly, Mum was frightened of nothing and nobody and when Charice threatened her, Mum retaliated and headbutted her.

"Mum wet herself in the shop, so she must have been really scared," Kylie said. "But she stood up for herself, just the same. You know what she's like, what she was like… She told Charice to leave her family alone. Mum and I walked back to my flat, but I'm on the second floor, and I spotted Charice walking towards us with a gang. I knew there was going to be trouble, but I had no idea how bad it would be. We heard them hammering on the door downstairs, shouting for us to go out."

Kylie explained Mum had initially wanted to call the police but had lost her own phone and Kylie's phone was broken.

With tears streaming down her face, Kylie said, "They were banging the door down and we couldn't ignore them for much longer. Mum went out to speak to them because she was protecting me, she was worried what they were going to do to me. I followed her down and she actually apologised to them. She said she was sorry for the row in the shop.

"The Gassman sisters were screaming threats and Mum stepped back, away from them. I was behind her and I said, 'Mum come on in'. I had no idea she'd been stabbed until she fell to the ground. The gang ran away, and people crowded round Mum. Someone tried to help her, tried to save her. I was frozen, trapped in a thick fog, like I was watching it all from outside my own body. I couldn't even go with Mum to hospital. When the police and paramedics came, I was taken away to make a statement. She went in the ambulance on her own and it broke my heart."

"You did your best," I comforted Kylie.

Mum had been left to die in a pool of blood, in the middle of a May afternoon, whilst shoppers and schoolchildren walked past. In death, as in life, she had been denied the dignity and respect she deserved and a hot fury bubbled under my skin. Next, I saw Cameron, who had turned 12 just a few weeks before Mum died. He explained he'd been due to see Mum at 3.30pm on the day of her death. He'd stood waiting, wondering where she was, unaware she had been stabbed 15 minutes earlier. Since he'd been taken into care, Mum had never been so much as a minute late for their meetings. Cameron had immediately sensed something was wrong.

"I was waiting for her outside school, and I just felt sick," Cameron told me. "I can't explain it."

"I did too," I told him, remembering how nauseous and disorientated I was at the call centre, around the time Mum had died. Her spirit had, in some way, connected and entwined with ours as it left this world. I felt so desolate, as if she had taken mine with her. Mum needed to be formally identified and with two of my sisters, I was taken to a police morgue, some way outside the town centre. Stepping inside, there was a pungent smell of antiseptic, so strong it stung the lining of my nose and throat.

It was dark and gloomy, with thick curtains across the doors. I was shown into a room to see Mum and instantly, I felt the temperature drop. I knew then that her energy was gone. She was covered with a sheet, but I was allowed to kiss her head and hold her hand. As a little girl, so many times, I'd longed for her to reach out and take my hand. But now that her hand was finally in mine, her fingers were stone cold. She was no longer here, and her hand was no longer hers. I stayed only a few more moments.

"When can I start making funeral plans?" I asked the officers.

"Not yet, sorry," they replied. "Your mother's body won't be released for some time yet. There will be at least one post-mortem."

As I left the morgue my heart rattled inside me; a collection of useless, broken pieces, never to be mended. I drove back home that same night, exhausted and yet strangely wired. The children went to school the next morning, but I called in sick at work. I could not face it. Walking into our empty house, the silence screamed at me. Gripping the edge of the banister, I turned and there was Grampy standing right in front of me. The morning sunshine reflected off his glasses. I saw the hairs on his forearms, exposed by his rolled-up sleeves. And then, that repugnant smell. It smacked at the back of my throat, and I retched into my palm.

"No!" I choked. "Not you! Get out!"

When I looked up, he had dissolved into a shaft of sunlight. But that image was burned onto my retinas. The memories flooded through my mind like a dam had burst.

"This is your fault!" I raged into the empty room. "All

yours! You abused Mum, you took away every last shred of her self-esteem. You stole the person she was supposed to be, and you left her with only a shell. That's why she took drugs, that's why she got into arguments, and she made the wrong choices. And that's why she was murdered."

I sank to the sofa and sobbed. I had no doubt in my mind that Grampy's abuse had caused Mum's death. He didn't push the blade through her skin. But in truth, he had been holding the knife over her right from the first time he raped her. Without the abuse, Mum would have been a different person completely. I reserved some blame for myself too. If I'd reported him, perhaps Grampy would have been jailed. Would that have been enough to save Mum, to show her that the abuse was not her fault? Her life could so easily have followed a different path. And now, it was too late.

"I'm sorry, Mum," I sobbed. "I'm so sorry."

The days that followed were a blur, marked out only by pain. I returned to Swindon to visit Mum in the funeral parlour, but again, I had no sense that she was there. Looking at her, I had again that familiar feeling that I was the parent and she was the daughter, and that I was here to mourn my own child.

"He will pay for this," I whispered. "I promise you that. We will get him in the end."

I saw now that Mum could never have had justice whilst she was alive. She was not strong enough to speak out herself, because Grampy had broken her. It was up to me, as it always had been, to look after her and to be her voice. The blazing sunshine, as I stepped outside, felt like a personal insult. Why was it not stormy, dark and gloomy? The world did not care enough to mourn with me. Once again, I felt myself falling into the role of the outcast. Everyone was against me.

That afternoon, I met with the police who told me Mum had been drug-tested as part of the murder investigation. My heart sank; it felt like they were going to use her addiction against her and blame her for her own murder. But the officer said, "Your mum was clean. Nothing at all in her system. She wasn't using drugs when she was killed."

My eyes widened and my chest swelled with pride. I had been sceptical when she confided, weeks before her death, that she was off drugs. But here was the proof that she was telling the truth.

"I am so proud of you," I whispered. "Well done."

Before the officer left, he said, "Is there anything you want to ask me, Tara?"

"Actually, yes," I replied, surprising even myself. "My mum was sexually abused by her father all through her childhood. It shaped the way she was, and I think it led to her death. Could you investigate him if I make the complaint?"

He sighed and shook his head.

"I'm sorry, but now that your mum is deceased, we'd have no chance of a conviction for historical sexual abuse."

It was what I'd expected but it was nonetheless another blow. I returned to Swindon and began planning Mum's funeral, which would take place at the end of June. Cameron came to live with us, his application fast-tracked by social services because of Mum's death. I hadn't seen so much of my youngest sibling as he grew up, but right from his arrival, we shared a strong, umbilical connection, as though I was back in the family bathroom, guiding him into the world.

Our love, embryonic and precious, grew day by day. He was more like my son than my little brother. Like me, he was lost in grief, and we leaned on each other. In the days before the funeral, I travelled back and forth to Swindon. I met with the police for an update on the case and asked again if Grampy could be prosecuted for what he had done to her.

"I don't think so," said the officer. "Your mother is no longer here to make a complaint."

"Well, I'm not giving up on it," I told him. "Mum deserves justice."

I tried to concentrate on the final funeral plans, but tensions crackled each time the family gathered. It was Father's Day that same week, and I'd bought Dad a nice aftershave. When he opened it, his face crumpled into an ugly frown.

"Is this all I'm worth to you?" he hissed. "A measly bottle of aftershave?"

I stared at him in disbelief. Dad hadn't bought me a present since I was a child. I had applied for a social services grant to pay for half of Mum's funeral, but I was meeting the remaining costs on my own. I had also agreed to pay for the whole wake single-handedly. On top of this, I was now a single mother of three children – one of whom was his own son.

Dad's lack of understanding and gratitude left me more disappointed than surprised. I was used to his behaviour, but still, though I glazed my heart against them, the words hurt. The night before the service, I made baby blue ribbons in Mum's memory for every mourner to wear. In the crematorium the next day, we played her favourite song, 'Close to You' by the Carpenters. I closed my eyes and saw her racing round the house with the hoover, spreading Shake n Vac on the bare floorboards.

"Love you, Mum," I whispered.

The chapel was filled with relatives and friends, but there was no sign of Grampy, and I was glad. Not even the devil could have had the audacity to turn up to Mum's funeral. He had put her in the coffin, just as the Gassmans had. I'd arranged Mum's wake for later that week. We stayed with Mum's brother the day before, and all afternoon, I was busy with preparations. I had ordered tablecloths and candles. I made several trips to the supermarket, to stock up on buffet food. The children were happy watching TV with my aunt whilst I buttered rolls in the kitchen. But halfway through opening a packet of ham, I was seized by a sudden clarity.

All those locked doors in my head burst open and rooms and corridors which I had kept airtight for so long merged into one big space. The truth burst to the surface like a swimmer coming up for air and I was left gasping with a strange mix of shock and relief. All my life, I'd played roles and I'd kept secrets. I had acted out the part which was demanded of me. Well, not anymore. It was time to be myself and shake the skeletons from their hiding places. It was not enough merely to let my mask slip. I wanted to rip it off and scream my secrets at the top of my lungs. Leaving the ham half-opened, I wiped my hands on a tea towel, grabbed my bag, and called, "Just nipping out. Won't be long."

"No problem, Tara," called my aunt.

I hurried along the pavement and with each step, a plan formulated in my mind. Mum wasn't here to testify against Grampy. So he'd have to testify against himself. It was the only way. I felt close to Mum, closer than I had even before her death, as I turned into Grampy's street. Justice became a portal to her; a way of connecting our two worlds. Right from that first time she confided in me, my life had been building towards this.

"You can do this, Tar," she whispered.

"I know," I said out loud. "And I will. I won't let you down."

17

BUT AS I reached the house, I faltered. The windows, unblinking, glared at me. I felt again those long invisible arms wrapping around me like rattlesnakes and pulling me in. The place was haunted, not by those ghosts from my childhood but by my own grandfather. He would be back soon from his evening visit to the pub, and the back door was unlocked as I'd known it would be. Like a ghost myself, I floated from room to room, stabs of nostalgia driving deeper with each moment. I remembered him pressing a pound coin into my palm. I felt myself hoisted into the air, onto his shoulders. I watched the bag of chocolate teacakes swinging from his arm.

You're so special, Tara, just like your mother. You're my girl.

I reached the bathroom and stuttered to a halt. Pain splintered through me like cracks across a frozen pond.

"This will pass," I reminded myself.

With a deep breath, I walked into the bathroom and leaned over to open the window. Even now, I had to have an escape route. I needed to hear my faithful friends, the birds. Outside the spare room, my skin prickled with shame. Memories ripped through me like shrapnel.

"I know I can rely on you, Tar," Mum said softly.

I could not let her down; she needed me now more than ever before. Downstairs, I sat on the edge of the sofa and waited, armed only with my phone and the truth. Childhood scenes played and replayed as though they were on mute on the TV in the corner. He still had the same TV stand. Underneath was a neatly stacked pile of videos: 'Elvis on Tour, 'The Best of Elvis,' 'Elvis Comeback special.' It was a sick lie, just like my whole childhood. When I heard the back door opening, I pressed record on my phone. Inexplicably, I felt calm. And Grampy, bizarrely, did not seem especially surprised to see me in his living room. It was almost as though our meeting, after years of estrangement, was a prior arrangement. The embodiment of all evil, he leaned against the doorframe. This monster had towered over my childhood. Yet he was so frail and stooped, he barely filled the doorway. I stared at him with a morbid fascination.

"I know, I know, I didn't go to the funeral," he said, wafting his hand impatiently as though he could simply sweep me away.

"Do you really think that's why I'm here, because you missed Mum's funeral?" I asked. "No. I'm here because you wrecked her life. You sexually abused her, didn't you right from being a small child?"

"Yes," he said, his head dropping. "I did."

I was blindsided by the instant confession. It was, again, as though he had been expecting me. His words sent shock-waves around the room, bouncing off the walls and the windows. Even Elvis seemed to drain of colour as he smirked at me from his hallowed position on the chimney breast.

"You admit, you sexually abused my mother?" I pressed.

"Yes," he said.

I didn't know whether he was capitulating out of remorse or disinterest and a rush of fury whipped through me. I took a deep breath. It was important to stay measured. I didn't want a defence barrister accusing me of forcing his confession.

"You abused me too, didn't you?" I continued, each syllable like a stain on my tongue.

"I did," he confirmed. "I'm sorry."

The inadequacy of the apology lit a fuse within me. I was angry for Mum, not for myself. I wanted vengeance and I wanted justice for her. Way up in the heavens, I wanted to make her proud of me at last.

"Sorry?" I hissed furiously. "Sorry? What use is that?"

I saw, again, the blood in the bath. I felt him yank my head down. I heard his hateful grunt. I smelled that appalling stench. Layer after layer of memory coalesced into rage.

"I'm recording this," I snapped, waving my phone. "And all you can say is sorry?"

"Yes," he nodded.

He appeared almost relieved to unburden himself of these secrets he had dragged around like Marley's chains all these years. I ended the recording. I had got what I'd come for.

"Mum was the best thing in my life, and you took her from me," I told him. "I blame you for it all. She would not have been murdered if you hadn't abused her. She would have been a different person altogether. I'm going to the police."

"You were always different, Tara," Grampy sighed, as I reached the door.

"Yes," I replied. "And here is the difference with me. I will see justice done."

Adrenaline racing, I marched out with my head held high as though I owned the whole street. But as I got around the corner, my legs gave way. Sinking to the ground, I sobbed and sobbed. Streaming alongside my fury was a strange and hollow sadness. Despite myself, I felt sympathy for Grampy. I could not help it. He looked so old and fragile. He had helped to raise me. Yet he had helped to ruin me too. He was my Grampy, and he was my abuser. How could both be possible? My heart and head in turmoil, I trudged home to continue making the sandwiches. I was annoyed with myself for worrying about Grampy. Yet this was who I was; I worried about everyone. There was no sense of celebration or victory at his confession; only a feeling of determination that I must see this to the end. His abuse had diminished Mum's light to the point where it had been completely extinguished, and the domino effect of his behaviour had spread like a deadly infection through the generations.

"It had to stop, Tar," Mum's spirit reminded me, as I wrapped each plate with clingfilm. "You broke that chain. You did it."

The wake, the following day, was a disaster. I was up before 6am, putting the finishing touches to the buffet food before carrying it over to the local social club. I'd rented a private room and even a Karaoke machine. I'd hoped, through Mum's love of music, singing might bring everyone together. I decorated the tables with flowers and candles and laid out the food and drinks.

"It looks beautiful," Jasmine told me, as she helped to unwrap the food. "We've done her proud."

Mourners gathered, but Grampy stayed away, as I had known he would. I tried to push his confession to the back of my mind and focus on what I was here for; to celebrate Mum's life. But it wasn't long before the mood soured. There were arguments between relatives and when a fight broke out, I quickly ushered the children outside. We drove straight back to Swansea rather than finding ourselves caught up in yet more trouble. As soon as we got home, I called the police.

"I'd like to make a report into historical sexual abuse," I said. "My mother and myself were both victims and I have a taped confession from the perpetrator."

I made an appointment to speak to an officer in person later that week. By that time, there had been a second complaint about Grampy. It was a punch to the gut to learn other children had suffered like me. But I was glad that another victim had come forward.

"If someone else is speaking out it means his hold over them is coming to an end," I said.

My police interview was harrowing. But it was empowering too. For years, I'd struggled to think clearly and to breathe deeply. Since I was a child, I'd dragged a weight along behind me like a suitcase filled with cement. I'd always thought it was the abuse. Now, I realise it was the secrets dragging me down. For as they floated to the surface, my breathing eased, and my burden grew lighter. Over the next few weeks, I was interviewed over and over, at different police stations and by different officers. I gave signed statements, video statements, additional statements. I had kept a copy of Grampy's confession, and I played it again and again. It was self-torture, but I couldn't seem to stop. Eventually, a friend insisted I delete it.

"Tara, you're not doing yourself any good," he said. "You need to let it go."

When an officer called to say Grampy would be charged with sexual abuse and rape against a number of children, I felt no relief or pleasure. I had no room for any other emotions than my all-consuming grief. As each day passed, I felt Mum's absence more and more and I was struggling to cope. As soon as the children were in bed each night, I opened a bottle of wine. I felt inexplicably frightened and vulnerable, so afraid of the darkness that I drank myself to sleep with the lights on, only to regain a groggy consciousness in the early hours. Waking up was like falling into an abyss of sadness. I watched myself, hurtling in freefall to certain death, but there was nothing I could do to stop it. There was no hand to reach out and pull me back.

In the mornings, I played a role, buttering toast, packing sandwiches, and chatting with the kids. I dressed as though I was off to work, but after dropping them at school, I slunk back home to cry. I did not know if I was trying to fool my children or myself. But there was no way I could have gone to work and I called in sick, day after day. Irrationally I convinced myself I could somehow resurrect Mum if I cried enough, if I showed the spirit world how much I wanted her back. I had, after all, always been so capable and practical, able to resolve all problems. So why couldn't I sort this?

I collected together Mum's belongings for a memory box: Her cardigan from the day she died. Two feathers I found in the garden when she was murdered. Two rings and a lock of her hair. From the cardigan, I had two pillows made, one for Cameron and one for me. It was not much to show for a life half-lived, and my heart broke all over again as I mourned the life she should have had and the legacy she should have left. I felt I would never heal. I dreaded each day but, as the months passed, I found some solace at night. Waking at around 4am one morning, I had a sense that Mum was with me. Just as I had known her spirit had left the morgue, I was certain she was here with me now.

Opening my eyes, I saw her sitting at the end of my bed, her eyes bright and her hair shining, just as she had been that day she was released from prison. She looked so beautiful. I was scared to reach out in case she melted away. But she took my hand and pulled me towards her. We hugged for so long; much longer than we had ever hugged when she was alive. I felt intense love from her, which, again, had been missing during her life. Transcending the boundaries of life and death, we were ironically closer than we had ever been before.

"Just please tell me you're safe," I whispered.

"Oh you don't need to worry about me, Tar," she smiled softly. "Not any more."

It was a relief to know she was no longer tormented. But in other ways, it made the needle of grief sharper still, because I wanted to get to know this new, gentle, version of my mother. I longed to feel the warmth of her arms around me again. One night, the lights flickered on and off as I lay in bed.

"Mum?" I asked, my heart flooded with hope. "Mum, is that you?"

So desperately, I wanted to believe that her spirit was with me. But in the deafening silence which followed, I questioned my own sanity. I felt, finally, as though I might be cracking. And this time, I could not see my way through the darkness.

18

THE TRIAL for Mum's murder was scheduled for November 2015 at Bristol Crown Court. Before it began, I had to tell my children something of the truth. They knew only that Mum had died, and not the circumstances. Before her murder, they understood they were not allowed to visit my parents on their own and that the relationship was difficult. They knew we never saw Grampy, and that they were not allowed to contact him. And as little children, they had accepted all of this without question. They grew up following specific rules and instructions, without understanding why. But the police warned Mum's murder trial would be covered in the media and so the time had come for me to be honest with them.

"Nan was taken away from us by two people who will go to prison for what they did," I explained. "And after the court case about Nan, there will be another one about Grampy. He abused Nan when she was little. He did bad things to her and to me too. That's why Nan took drugs, and she made bad choices, because she was very sad inside. I hope Grampy will be punished for what he did to me and Nan."

Brandon and Shania cuddled up either side of me on the sofa. Whilst they were too young for the details of what had happened, they understood I had suffered in some way. The warmth of their arms around me was the best therapy I could have wished for. I was relieved to get the explanation of the way; I didn't like hiding things from them.

My own childhood had been about secrets, and theirs had to be different. But oddly, after I spoke with them, I was awash with shame. I felt as though I was letting them down because I couldn't give them the extended family they deserved. Their friends had grandparents, great-grandparents, aunts, uncles and cousins. Our family was just us three; precious but tiny. I dreamed, always, of the ideal and without fail I fell short.

The trial came around quickly, and I arranged to travel to Bristol by car with Mum's brother. I hadn't had much contact with him growing up; he didn't see eye to eye with my dad, as most people didn't. But now that Mum was dead, he was doing his best to support me, and I was glad to have him by my side.

Preparing to face Mum's killers for the first time was daunting, but I had to do it for her. I had tried, in the days before, to prepare myself for that moment when we locked eyes. I kept on reminding myself to stay calm and measured in the presence of such wickedness. But as I walked into the courtroom, I was blindsided. The two sisters, Amberstasia and Charice, were leaning back against the glass surround of the dock and waving at family members in the public gallery above. One of them was smiling and making funny gestures with her hands. A burst of fury whistled through me.

My thoughts were on short-circuit. My whole body buzzed with shock. I'd prepared myself for many things but not this. They were so casual, so flippant, so frivolous. I might just have walked into a youth club, not a murder trial. Once again, as in life and in death, Mum was not shown the respect and dignity she deserved. As I took my seat, my anger bubbled and fizzed.

Both sisters denied murder, and Charice admitted manslaughter. On that first day as the prosecution outlined the case, Charice Gassmann, then 19, was described in court as a 'bully out for revenge' who enlisted her sister Amberstasia, 23, to ambush Mum. The jury was told the attack came in May 2015 after Kylie had discovered a bike covered in brown sauce outside her front door.

Later, witnesses heard Charice taunting and goading Mum to fight with her in the local shop. Mum had defended herself and headbutted Charice but was so afraid she had wet herself. Mum went back to Kylie's flat, but the sisters stormed after her, hammering on the door, and threatening to: 'f****** kill her.' When Mum came outside moments later, she suffered a single fatal knife wound to the right side of her chest. The blade, measuring at least eight inches, pierced her heart. Though paramedics battled to save her, she was declared dead in hospital. The sisters fled the scene in a black car which was waiting for them; Charice was taken to hospital, whilst Amberstasia returned to her flat and smoked a spliff. Alastair Malcolm, prosecuting, said, "Charice Gassmann was being aggressive in the Premier store. She started it but came out worse. She was acting like a bully but like a number of bullies, when they come off worse that spurs them on. What she did after was revenge. She armed herself with a knife, but also she went there to have the help of her sister. They went back together so that they could carry out revenge on Alison Connolly for having the audacity to hit Charice in the Premier store."

One witness heard Charice tell her sister: "Get my machete." Another heard one of the sisters say: "I'm going to smash her f****** head in."

Mum went outside to try to calm them down and was told by Amberstasia, "'I'm going to batter you, don't you dare touch my sister."

After Mum was stabbed, a witness recalled Amberstasia saying, "That's what happens if you f**k with my family". Another witness heard Charice shout that she was: "going to get done for murder".

That same afternoon, the CCTV of Mum's death was shown on a large screen in court. My blood ran cold as the images flickered into life. I'd seen the film many times before, but this was so public and so raw. And this time, in the same room as the CCTV, were the killers themselves, brought back, quite literally, to the scene of the crime. After Mum fell to the floor, the trees around her continued to sway in the spring breeze, and it was another cruel reminder of how life was continuing without her, and how the two women who had taken her life away were still smirking and laughing, nodding at their relatives as though they were proud of the film. I heard myself wailing and screaming, and I felt an arm on mine.

"Stop," said an usher in my ear. "Try and calm down."

But her words just infuriated me further.

"Me?" I yelled. "Why should I calm down? My mother's killers are laughing at us! Tell them, not me!"

My whole body was alight with a rage which scared me. I fled the court, sobbing and shouting, with the usher close behind.

"You don't need to go back inside, just take some time," she said.

But I shook my head. It was tempting to close my eyes, to fly away, with the little birds outside. But had to go back into court, for Mum. I had to show them I would not be broken.

"This will pass," I told myself. "Tomorrow will come."

Back in court, I heard how Charice had ongoing mental health and anger issues including 'voices' in her head. She told the court she had smoked cannabis every day as a coping mechanism. She even admitted she had thoughts about stabbing people who made her angry and said the thoughts scared her.

"I just started smoking cannabis when I was 14 to deal

with it," she said. "When I started it was just for fun, but it dulled my brain. If I do not smoke, I get angry and really agitated."

She also claimed to hear voices in her head and said: "One of them is sarcastic and the other one is just angry. At times it is not just thoughts, and I am actually hearing them. One is deeper than the other, so I think of the other as female. Some are deep and rough, and the others are calm and collected, but more sarcastic. They just kick in whenever they feel like it, near enough every day. I just try to block it out. I have given them names so I can tell the difference. The female tries to calm me down, but the male tries to wind me up. I smoke cannabis because I find it easier to block them out and not to listen."

Amberstasia claimed not to know her sister had a knife and said she did not even realise at first that Mum had been stabbed. But the court had previously heard from witnesses who saw Amberstasia punch Mum to the head after she had been stabbed, saying "that's what happens when you f*** with my family".

The CCTV showed Amberstasia moving towards Mum before making physical contact.

"You lunge towards her twice," said Mr Malcolm. "The truth is you knew your sister had a knife and that she was going to 'nank' somebody with it."

Amberstasia said she had thought Mum was lying when she shouted that she had been stabbed.

"When she said she had been stabbed I did say, 'no you haven't'," she admitted.

Reliving Mum's final moments, day after day, was torture. Worse still was the lack of remorse or regret from the Gassmans. Their flippancy was a cruelty all of its own. This all seemed like one big joke to them. The hearing was listed for three weeks and so I split my time between doing school runs and bedtime stories in Swansea and attending the court in Bristol. Whilst I tried to keep a semblance of normality for the children, it was almost impossible.

Our lives were descending into exactly the sort of chaos I had vowed to avoid. Into the third and final week of the trial, I realised it was time to pull back. The children needed to get back to school full-time, and we were all missing home. On December 14, a police liaison officer called to tell me Charice had been convicted of murder and jailed for life. Amberstasia had been cleared of murder but convicted of manslaughter and sentenced to 12 years. I didn't know how to feel as I ended the call. I was numb. My jagged-edged fury at the trial had burned itself out, leaving behind an empty husk. It made little difference to me how long Mum's killers would serve, because nothing would bring her back.

"I'm sorry, Mum," I said softly.

But even my apology felt useless. The next day, I read the final reports in the local papers. The jury of eight men and four women had chosen not to accept Charice acted due to a loss of self-control or a personality disorder. The court heard she had previous convictions for violence including biting the face of a 14-year-old. Murderer Charice Gassmann, 19, was told she must serve at least 19 years before she could be considered for parole. Amberstasia, 23, was told she must serve half of her 12-year term for manslaughter before being considered for parole. Judge Graham Cottle said, "There was premeditation there, a period of 10 minutes between the initial headbutt and the stabbing. You went over and armed yourself with a knife, you had violent intentions, to cause serious harm to Alison Connolly. You both were aware that violence was about to happen. You wanted to settle a score. Get revenge for what she had done to you. And you carried that out."

Judge Cottle condemned Charice's lack of remorse in the killing.

"You sent me a letter telling you were remorseful. Watching you over the weeks I have seen few signs of genuine remorse. All I have seen is signs of anger and irritability as you dealt with questions."

Reading the judge's comments sent me into despair. More than anything, I'd wanted Mum's killers to show accountability. I had hoped, albeit naively, they might be regretful or sorry. But from what I had seen, they were not. The end of the trial served only to hammer home the message that Mum was dead, and to cement her place in the past. I could not bear to think I would never see her again. Her spirit continued to appear to me at night, but even this was bittersweet. In ephemeral, dream-like moments, I believed she was with me; I smelled her shampoo, I saw her eyes crinkle as she smiled. And every morning, the illusion was smashed.

"Mum, please come back," I begged. "Please. I let you down, I promise it won't happen again. I will be there for you."

In February 2015, just two months after the trial had ended, I received a letter to say the Gassman sisters had lodged an appeal. Charice Gassman was appealing both her conviction and sentence. Amberstasia was appealing her sentence. Again, I was swallowed up by despair. Bad enough that they had lied throughout the trial, that they had laughed and joked as Mum's murder was shown in court. Now, they wanted to wriggle out of the punishment. Again, it seemed as though the whole thing was a game to them, something to stretch out for as long as they could. But just seeing their names printed on the letter sent me lunging back into the past. I saw, again, Mum's crumpled body as she bled to death. I saw the trees waving gently in the breeze. I relived it all. Why could they not just leave us alone? That night, the appeal was covered on the TV and in the local papers. The Gassmans' police mugshots were on the TV. The CCTV of Mum's murder resurfaced online. I closed my eyes, wishing I could somehow lock all this away, as I had as a child. Instead, the whole world seemed to be talking about it.

"They won't win the appeal," I reassured Jasmine, when she called that night. "Don't worry."

"That's not the point," she replied. "They shouldn't put us through this."

19

THERE WERE 13 months between the two trials, but the time was sucked into a matter of weeks. Life was a blur on fast-forward, and Monday became Friday so quickly that I could not keep up. I felt like time was running away from me, as though it no longer wanted to be a part of my trauma. I remembered how slowly time had dragged when I was a child; how 15 minutes locked in the toilet block at primary school had felt like hours. How those weekends at Grampy's had lasted a lifetime. How those nights comforting my siblings whilst our home was raided were never-ending. Yet in what felt like less than a month, an officer called to run through my witness statement about my grandfather.

"I'm not sure I can do it," I mumbled. "I'm really not."

"Have a think about it," the officer said.

But I was still getting over Mum's murder trial. How could I possibly give evidence at Grampy's trial? He had been charged with sexually abusing several children between the ages of four and 14, over a 40-year period. I'd hoped he might plead guilty and show a small shred of decency. He had admitted attempted rape and two counts of indecent assault on one victim, but was continuing to deny four counts of rape, seven of indecent assault, one of indecency with a child and one of indecent assault of a child. Days before the trial was due to start, my phone bleeped with a text from an unknown number.

'You're disgusting,' read the message. 'Why are you putting an old man in jail?'

I knew this had to be from a relative; someone close to both Grampy and me. Reeling, I blinked away tears. The next day, from a different number, a message read: 'Happy with yourself, putting your own grandfather behind bars?'

I'd been putting up with abuse of one form or another for all of my life and I had learned to insulate against it. But the worst part was, I had those same concerns. He was old, frail and weak. And he was my Grampy. He'd bought me chocolate teacakes, taken me to Blockbuster, and carried me on his shoulders. With Grampy, I'd felt like I mattered, for a short time at least. How could I help to jail him? If he had been horrible to me all of the time, my choice would have been so much easier.

The dilemma was cruel – which was exactly what he had intended. That's why he'd got away with such vile behaviour all his adult life. Over two sleepless nights I wrestled with the decision. Even the night before, I wavered back and forth. I dropped the children at school and then, almost as if I was guided by a higher force, I went to the train station.

I found myself outside Swindon Crown Court, completely alone but completely determined. With razor-sharp focus, I knew I had to break the chain, for Mum, and for me. This was my moment to fix the family. I had spent my childhood trying to heal us all and finally, my chance was here. The solution lay before me, as clear and hard as crystal. With my legs trembling, suspended somewhere between two equal horrors, I was taken to wait in a witness room. A liaison officer offered me coffee, but I shook my head. I couldn't even swallow, I was so nervous.

When my name was called, my stomach turned. I thought I was going to throw up. As I walked into the court, caught somewhere between terror and grief, the only sound I heard was my own blood pounding through my ears. Everything else was almost inaudible. Grampy, old, frail and bald, looked so out of place in the dock. I reminded myself it was him, not me, who had put him there. His outward appearance didn't matter; he had taken innocent children and broken them into small pieces.

Grampy was known to us all as Mark, but in court he appeared under the name Martin. I'd never heard the name in my life, but then, he was a man with many secrets. As I took my place in the witness box, my heart clattered against my ribs. The walls seemed to shrink around me, closing in until I was fighting for oxygen. For a second, I was back in the bath, aged six. I heard the lock click as Grampy closed the door. Another flash, and I was on stage at the strip club, quivering with fear. I hated being under the spotlight, parading my darkest secrets for all the world to see. Yet here I was again.

"I can see that you're nervous," said the prosecution barrister kindly. "Please, have a sip of water and take a moment."

Turning to the jury, he explained that just a few months earlier, I'd attended a murder trial for my mother, who was also one of the victims in the sexual abuse case. I was grateful for his compassion. But when the defence barrister stood to question me, he said, "We all appreciate you've been through a very traumatic year. Do you feel capable of answering questions in this court today?"

As he spoke, my anxiety was displaced by indignation.

"Yes," I said firmly. "I'm perfectly capable. I'm upset, not insane."

Reliving the attacks, through cross-examination, was painful. I felt like a walking wound; my pain exposed for all to see. My childhood was at once distant and yet horribly close. Too close. I was asked in detail about the recording I'd made and why I'd chosen to do it, after so long.

"For my mother," I said simply. "I did it for her."

As the questioning continued, I grew in confidence. And as my questioning drew to a close, I drew in a breath and turned to face Grampy.

"You knew I was different," I told him. "It stops now. It all stops now."

After my evidence, I travelled straight home. I had done

what I set out, and I could take no more. I followed the case online, recoiling as I read testimonies from other victims, scarily similar to mine. He had groomed young children, starting with watching explicit videos, buying them sweets and giving them money, before moving on to sexual assaults and, in some cases, rape. In their teens, he had plied them with booze and cigarettes.

Now, more than ever, I was sure of my decision. The only place for a monster like this was prison. Not just for Mum, or for me, but for the safety of all children. Part-way through his trial, Grampy admitted more of the allegations, but continued to deny the others. He claimed he had drink and drug addictions and mental health issues. I had never once seen him take drugs and I didn't believe it. He claimed also to have worked hard all his life, as a builder and a kitchen porter. But I could not remember him ever having a job. Enmeshed in a tissue of his own lies, I doubted he even knew what the truth was.

By the end of the trial, he had changed his plea again and admitted all but one of the charges. He pleaded guilty to three counts of rape, one attempted rape, 11 indecent assaults and gross indecency on five vulnerable children. One charge of rape was left to lie on file. I felt nothing but disgust at his last-minute attack of conscience. It was far too little, too late, and no doubt self-serving. On January 12, 2017, he was jailed for 19 years.

Judge Tim Mousley QC said, "This was sustained,

systematic, gross abuse of vulnerable young children. It included rape. There was grooming and that included attempts by you to get, some of them at least, to watch pornography. I detect no remorse in you whatsoever… The impact on each one of them has been profound and it will last forever, to some extent. In relation to each of them: they were innocent children."

It was accepted that, at the age of 77, he would die in prison. Even when the police called later that day to confirm his sentence, it still did not feel real. The next morning, Grampy's face and his hateful crimes were plastered all over the media. I wish I could say I felt only relief. But the usual imposters of guilt and shame somehow burrowed their way in too. There was nobody there to support me, nobody to tell me I'd done the right thing.

Instead, our family was more viciously divided than ever before, and there was a line of relatives waiting to condemn me for jailing an old man. It was no wonder that I blamed myself and that I questioned what was right. I had been brainwashed and groomed, not only by Grampy, but by some members of my wider family, who believed a prolific paedophile should walk free. Mine was one of the most messed-up families in the world. Our secrets had been buried for so long but now they were pasted on billboards for all to see. They might just as well have been projected onto the night sky in neon lights. I hardly knew which was worse; filthy secrets or brutal exposure. That night, Mum came to me in a dream and asked, "Why did you put my father in prison? Why did you do it, Tara? I told you not to go to the police but you did it anyway. Why?"

I woke, choking on my sobs, with sweat running between my shoulder blades. The weight of blame lay on my chest like a brick and made it impossible for me to move.

"I'm sorry," I croaked. "I'm really sorry, Mum. But I did this for you. I hope you can see that one day."

Some months after losing Mum, I'd met a man named Christian. I didn't want a relationship and at first, we were just friends. But Christian was patient and understanding and, though I expected him to run a mile at each new horrifying revelation, he stuck around. He had a traditional, loving family which must have made my situation all the more mind-boggling for him. One night, we let off lanterns in Mum's memory. Other nights, he listened as I raged against the Gassman sisters, or I persecuted myself for putting Grampy in jail.

"Tara, you did the right thing," he told me. "Deep down, you know that. Be proud of yourself."

But even his kind words could not reach me. In the months after Grampy's trial, I felt myself slipping further and further away, as though I was clinging to a rope dangling over the edge of a cliff. One night I woke, sweating and shaking, in the middle of a nightmare. Grampy was so close; I could hear him grunting, I could smell him. With my heart pounding, I flicked the torch on my phone. The pillow next to me was suddenly illuminated and sure enough, where Christian should have been sleeping, it was Grampy.

"Get out!" I screamed. "Get out of my bed! What are you doing here?"

I jumped out of bed, tangled in the duvet, and cowered in the corner, still shining my torch; a light not strong enough to guide me to safety.

"Tara, what's wrong?" Christian asked, sitting bolt upright. "Why are you shouting? What time is it?"

In that moment, Grampy was gone, dissolving, ghoul-like, into the ether. I didn't know how to tell Christian I had mistaken him for a paedophile. I understood it was a hallucination. But it was also painfully, horribly real.

"It's okay," Christian soothed, when he saw my tears. "Come back to bed. You're safe."

He held out his hands, but even then, my eyes darted to his wrist, to see if he was wearing Grampy's watch. I no longer knew what was real and what was not.

"No, I'm going downstairs for a cup of tea," I said warily. "You go back to sleep."

I felt like I was losing my mind.

In December 2017, we got news that both appeals by the Gassman sisters had failed. But the news did nothing to cheer me up and hearing their names again was a sharp rake over the embers of my grief. It was no comfort to me that they were in prison.

The New Year came, and I wasn't sleeping or eating properly.

Each morning, I went through the pretence of dressing in a smart work suit and a pair of heels whilst I chatted happily to the children over breakfast and walked them to school. Afterwards, I got changed back into my pyjamas and cried until it was time for school pick up. I thought I was fooling everyone. But one morning, as she pushed her cereal around the dish, Shania said to me, "Mummy are you okay? Why are you sad?"

With a whoosh, I was thrown back in time to see my mother, hunched over her mattress, weeping softly as my six-year-old self held a damp facecloth to her head.

What's wrong, Mum? Why are you sad?

The scene swirled and swam before my eyes and when the image reconfigured, I saw that I was the one on the mattress and Shania was holding the facecloth. The parallel tore through me like an electric shock. With my head in my hands, I realised what I was becoming. I had vowed, always, that I would not become my mother. That my children would not become another me. I had promised not to crush them with that same burden. As a little girl, I had never believed I was enough to make my mother smile. I was not loved enough. I was not loveable enough. I just was not enough. My own children could not carry that through life as I had. As Shania stirred her cereal, I put one arm around her, the other around Brandon, and said, "I'm not okay, you're right, and I'm glad you've noticed. I am really sad at the moment. I am sad because Nan died, and I am sad because of what

Grampy did. But I promise you I will get better. I won't be sad forever."

The relief spread like warm sunlight through our kitchen. Shania put down her spoon and stretched her arms around me.

"Good," she said. "I want you to get better."

It was wrong, I realised, to have masked my pain, to have lived a lie and expected them to accept it. Before we left for school, I ran upstairs to change into my jeans.

"I'm not going to work today," I announced. "I'm having some time at home whilst I get better."

Just by telling the truth, I felt 10 times lighter than before. And already, I knew that I would make it back, 10 times stronger than before. My recovery was slow, but I tried to be patient with myself. I made plans to meet friends for coffee. I took the kids out to the cinema. My employers had been very supportive, and I called my boss and arranged to go back to work part-time. And when I was sad, I no longer squirrelled myself away under my duvet. I cried in front of the children, and I told them I was struggling. It was important, especially for Cameron, that they understood crying was a strength, and not a weakness.

"We'll get through this together," I told them.

Whether I fought against it or not, I realised the Gassmans would have a presence in my life forever. And so, I made an application through the prison service to visit them. I accepted I didn't know their story, just as they didn't know ours. As a child, I'd learned a valuable lesson never to judge anyone. I was an advocate for people who struggled with life, and I'd battled for Mum and my siblings on that basis for many years. It was time, I realised, to open my heart to the Gassman sisters too. There was nothing they could do or say which would hurt me; I was self-taught in survival, and though they had tried to destroy me, they had failed. They had shown no compassion. So it was up to me to do it for them.

"I don't want to shout at them or judge them," I told the liaison worker who called me. "I just want to hear their story."

A couple of weeks later, I got a letter to say the sisters had refused to meet with me. I was disappointed but not surprised. Meeting me was a very small gesture they could have made, one tiny step on the road to redemption and apology. I had offered them that chance and I could do no more. But afterwards, something inside me changed, matured almost, like a flower coming into bloom. There was no point in me carrying around anger, pain and resentment. Life was too short for those negative emotions, as I knew only too well. And so, I forgave Charice and Amberstasia Gassman. And with that forgiveness, peace settled on me, like one of the little birds on my shoulder.

20

THROUGH THE police, I'd been offered counselling after Mum's murder. I found it so moving, in a group setting, to hear what other people had been through. And it helped too. My own healing was in listening, not speaking. At the end of the sessions, I was asked if I would consider meeting with other families who had lost a loved one to murder.

"Yes of course," I agreed. "I'd like to help wherever I can."

My friends raised their eyebrows when I announced I was off to London to help counsel another family.

"Tara, you should be getting help yourself, not helping others," they said. "When are you ever going to put yourself first?"

But I just smiled. I'd been looking after people for as long as I could remember and for me, that was therapy in itself. In London, I met with a poor mother whose small child had been murdered by her partner. It was the most horrific thing I had ever heard.

"I am so sorry," I told her. "I really am."

I was overawed by her courage and strength, just to keep

going, from day to day. Losing a child was the worst trauma imaginable for any parent. And, as I waited to catch my train home, I felt so blessed and fortunate. It was an honour to be rushing home, dashing out of the train station and onto the bus, so I was back in time for the school bell. That poor mother had helped me to heal, and I hope I helped her too. I think of her so often. That night, I hugged Cameron, Brandon and Shania close to me.

"We're so lucky," I told them. "We have each other, and this is all we need."

From then, I decided to follow a career in caring. I was good at shouldering other people's problems, at lightening the load of those who could not carry it alone. In 2019, I got a job as a support worker in a mental health unit. The following year, I lost my job when the Covid lockdown hit. After a few months at home, schooling the kids and refereeing their squabbles, I got a new role working in drug and alcohol services. Day to day, I was supporting addicts and ex-addicts, and I related well to them, as they did to me. Even without knowing my background, there was a connection, an invisible thread, which connected us. Surprisingly, it was the other staff members, not the clients, who I clashed with. I didn't like the way they spoke about our service users.

"They're not just addicts, they're people," I reminded them. "They're someone's child, someone's mum or dad. Try and remember that. They deserve the same respect as you and me."

Eight months on, I spotted a promotion, working in Swansea Prison, facilitating contact between families and offenders. It was a cause close to my heart, and I loved knowing that I was the bridge keeping parents and children connected. One year on, I was offered a job at a different prison working with youth offenders. This was more challenging with more responsibilities, and I was pleased with the direction my career was heading. I'd been at the prison about a year when I was asked to take part in a group exercise about knife crime. I filed into a conference room with around 30 colleagues. After listening to speakers, we were divided into groups for role play, where one half would run at the others with plastic knives. My heart seemed to jump a little every time someone said 'knife' but I tried to ignore it. Then, as we were moving the tables and chairs, ready for the role play, I came out in a cold, shivery sweat.

"Are you okay, Tara?" one of my colleagues asked. "You're shaking."

Numbly, I nodded. I took my place at one side of the room. But as I saw the knife coming towards me, I was suddenly catapulted back in time to Mum's murder. I was outside Kylie's flat, watching as Mum fell bleeding to the ground. My colleague had morphed into Charice Gassman. And the plastic knife he held was now a deadly blade. The walls seemed to crowd in on me. Gasping, I fell to the floor, clutching at my chest. I couldn't breathe. I couldn't speak. I was so afraid. My chest was so tight, I thought I was having a heart attack. I must have blacked out for a few moments because when I came round, the room was cleared. I was propped up with cushions, with a blanket over my legs.

"Tara, are you okay?" asked one of my colleagues. "We've called the first aiders. They'll be here soon."

"I'm sorry," I stuttered. "I don't know what's wrong with me."

By the time the first aiders arrived, I was starting to feel much better. My breathing was regular, and I had stopped shaking.

"We think you had a panic attack," they said.

As always, my first thought was to blame myself.

"I'm so sorry," I repeated. "I feel so embarrassed."

The first aiders assured me it wasn't my fault, and that a panic attack was a normal physiological reaction to stress.

"You can't help that," they said. "Don't be so hard on yourself."

But the shame stuck in my throat like a sticky ball of glue. When I was feeling strong enough, I went to the bathroom and locked myself in. Once again, time rewound, and I was a small child hiding in a toilet cubicle, panicking that my mother might die whilst I was at school. I had worried so much about her, and in the cruellest of self-fulfilling prophecies, she was now dead. Just like the panic attack, I felt this was my fault too. Facing my colleagues later, I was mortified. I'd tried so hard to block my personal traumas out of my career, but it hadn't worked. That week, I began to feel panicky on my morning commute. Approaching the prison, I came out in a cold sweat. One morning, I had to pull over and take deep breaths. At work, I worried constantly that I was going to have another panic attack.

"I just can't do this anymore," I admitted.

Though my bosses were supportive, I conceded a prison was not the right working environment for me. There were too many harmful triggers lurking behind every door. My panic attack was a set-back, but I was determined it would not hold me back for long.

"This will pass," I reminded myself. "Tomorrow is coming."

Like the hailstorm which had reduced us to tears on the school run, I tried to use the experience to spur me onwards. I reminded myself that life knocked me down so that I could get back up again, stronger than before.

In May 2021, I received a letter from the prison service and even before I opened it, I had guessed the contents. Amberstasia Gassman had served the minimum six-year term of her sentence, and she was about to be released. A wave of sadness engulfed me, knocking me backwards. I sank on to a chair as my tears pooled. I had worked hard to quell my anger towards the Gassmans. I had forgiven them. But that didn't mean I was comfortable with Amberstasia Gassman walking the streets again. At just 29 years old, she was a young woman with her life ahead of her. Mum was in a box, in my living room, with her life snatched from her. I didn't know the answer for dealing with violent criminals. But I knew it was not this. Again, I worked hard to keep myself from slipping into a depression. Like a stone in my shoe, the grief was always there. But I was learning, slowly, to hobble along regardless.

21

DAD AND I had been at loggerheads since I'd left for Swansea, and even after Mum's murder, there was animosity between us. He seemed to turn his anger outwards towards others. But in the years following the trial, his health hit a downward slide. He was diagnosed with spinal cancer and cobstructive pulmonary disease (COPD) and quickly became weak and vulnerable. I called him regularly to check on him.

"How are you getting to the hospital for your appointments?" I asked him.

"Oh, I'll manage," he told me. "Don't worry about me."

"I'll take you," I offered. "It's no problem at all."

When my family needed me, I had to be there. It was part of my make-up and I was learning, at last, to see that as a positive trait. Even in the months since I'd last seen him, Dad had deteriorated. Always skinny, he was painfully thin, and his skin had a grey tinge. Still addicted, he was using illicit drugs as painkillers. In the waiting room at the hospital, we chatted more easily than we ever had.

He seemed genuinely interested in news about Cameron, Brandon and Shania.

"I'd love to see them again," he told me, and then, with his voice breaking, "I know I don't deserve to. I don't deserve you either."

My own eyes stung with tears as I reached for his hand. It was the first time Dad had ever accepted responsibility or accountability for his behaviour. Like an ice cap melting, there was suddenly a closeness between us and a willingness, from me, to put the past behind us and enjoy whatever time we had left. True to my word, I took the children to see him the following weekend. There was some conflict in taking them back into an environment we had once fled. But I also recognised they deserved to get to know my father before he died.

"Remember, Grandad's behaviour is not the sort of behaviour we have at home," I told them. "But he's sick, so we're here to cheer him up."

Dad was in obvious pain and the house, as always, reeked of cannabis. But he made a big effort with the kids. His remorse was genuine; I could see that. After we arrived back in Swansea that evening, Dad texted: 'I am sorry about everything, Tara.'

Those six words were balm to my soul. I had waited all my life for that apology.

'It's okay,' I replied. 'It's all forgotten.'

I continued to take him for scans and treatment. But his

doctors warned his outlook was not hopeful. He began using crack cocaine and, as he was gripped by a dark addiction, he descended into mental turmoil. Sometimes, he'd text in the early hours telling me he was suicidal and could take no more. In those lonely moments before dawn, I talked him back into a place where he was loved.

'Tomorrow is coming,' I told him. 'Things always look better in the morning.'

Other times, he'd text with apologies about the way he'd treated me. Some nights, he even sent snippets of poetry he was writing. He composed a beautiful poem about a flower blossoming. Much of his poetry focussed on how bad he felt and how sorry he was. Another night, he sent excerpts from his favourite artists, Enya and Pink Floyd.

'Don't dwell on the past,' I told him.

Back at the hospital, his consultant reiterated that he was deteriorating. He warned Dad would need to change his lifestyle, and give up smoking, to allow the treatment to work. But Dad, despite his physical frailty, was stubborn as ever on the inside. And in a way, it was a relief to see that his old spirit was still there. At his next chemotherapy appointment, he was allowed a short break before hooking up to the drip. I thought he was going outside for a cigarette. My jaw dropped when, right there in the hospital grounds, he slipped a small purple bong out of his pocket and proceeded to get stoned.

"Dad, you are just not taking this seriously?" I asked him, aware my words were an enormous understatement.

But he just winked at me and puffed on his bong. He would never change, and maybe now, it was too late anyway. One sunny afternoon in July 2022, I took the day off work, and we went to see Dad.

It was always hard, returning to Swindon. Every time we passed the 'Welcome to England' sign, I felt a wave of nausea. I knew I was closer to Grampy's house. I was nearing the place Mum had been murdered. I was nearer to Amberstasia Gassman. All my time spent with Dad was smeared with dread as one memory after another was regurgitated. I had no choice but to swallow them down again and plaster on a smile. But when we arrived in Swindon, Dad was down in the dumps. Unusually for him, he had no money, and his kitchen cupboards were empty.

"Come on," I said, picking up my car keys. "I'll get you some shopping."

Walking into Asda, I was nipped by so many reminders from the past. I'd been here aged nine, shoplifting a pregnancy test when I feared I might have become pregnant through watching pornography. And I suppressed a nostalgic smile as I remembered Mum popping my spot cream into her pocket as we swept up and down the aisles on a shoplifting spree. In her own way, she had done her best. Along with a weekly shop, we bought a big pizza to share back at Dad's. After he'd eaten and we'd caught up on news, he seemed a bit brighter. He walked outside to wave us goodbye, and in my rear-view mirror I saw him brush away one lonely tear.

'I'm worried about you,' I texted. 'Please don't be sad. We all love you.'

But he didn't reply. The following evening, one of my sisters called to say Dad had been taken into hospital. I called the ward immediately and a doctor told me he'd had a suspected stroke.

"I'll book the day off work tomorrow," I said. "Please let him know I'll be there as soon as I've taken the kids to school."

The next morning, I was up early, making plans to set off for Swindon after the school run. But before I left the house, the phone rang.

"I'm so sorry, your father died during the night," said a nurse. "I held his hand."

Choked, I could only mumble my thanks. Hoisting my grief to one side, I felt guilty, as usual. I had promised to be there for him. He had pushed me away all my life and yet despite our reconciliation, he had died alone. It felt so cruel. Our relationship had, in many ways, been only in its infancy. Ours were only the green shoots of love. And so, I grieved for the father I did not have and for the bond we did not share. I grieved the lack and not the love. Dad's funeral was held at the same crematorium as Mum's. As with Mum, I organised it on my own and set up a payment plan with the funeral directors. I was still paying off Mum's funeral when Dad died – a tragedy on so many levels. The service itself was not what I had hoped. Several mourners arrived worse for wear, and I struggled to concentrate on my grief because of the chaos around me. Months later, an inquest ruled that Dad had died after a stroke caused by crack cocaine. The hearing heard Dad had been taken to hospital by ambulance after he became unwell and unresponsive due to the drug. At Swindon and Wiltshire Coroner's Court, the coroner Ian Singleton heard that Dad, who was just 57 years old, had suffered a bleed on the brain following a specific type of stroke which often immediately followed the use of crack cocaine. I was horrified, the following day, to see Dad's inquest reported in the local newspapers, and the story was quickly passed around on social media. With the bare facts, Dad was portrayed as just another drug addict, just another sad soul. I wished the journalist had reached out so that I could have offered some balance and humanity to his writing. I was so angry that I called the reporter myself.

"People are not just numbers. They are not faceless druggies, alkies or losers," I snapped. "They all have their story. They all have their struggles. They all deserve dignity."

Dad was a drug addict; that was true. But he was a person too.

One morning in October 2022, Jasmine called and, from her voice I knew instantly something was wrong.

"What is it?" I asked.

She took a deep breath.

"It's Grampy," she said. "He's dead."

He was an elderly man, 82 years old, and he'd gone

into prison already suffering from angina and other heart problems. This should not have been unexpected. But her words winded me. I clutched the doorframe, as though the floor might open up beneath me.

"Okay, thanks," I stuttered. "Thanks for letting me know."

As I'd feared, it wasn't long before a stream of vitriol was running through my phone.

'He died in prison because of you.'

'He was an old man. You took away his final years.'

'Shame on you.'

The messages were from the very people who ought to have supported me. Still, after all this time, I could not make sense of them choosing him over his victims. The messages left me cold. And yet, they could not hurt me more than I hurt myself. I did not care what bile they directed at me, but I hated to think that Mum would be disappointed in me, and as I deleted each message, guilt bloomed like mould in my heart. I had sent my own Grampy, the same man who had bought me Jaffa cakes and read me stories, to die in a cell. Just as I had studied Mum's behaviours when I was small, I asked myself how and why he had become a paedophile. The amateur psychologist in me had a need to try to understand his psyche, but perhaps also it was my way of avoiding facing who he really was and what he had done. There were no reasons, no excuses, no explanations. He was beyond all redemption and forgiveness. And deep down, I knew that. But that night, Mum's voice invaded my nightmares.

"I asked you not to do this, Tara," she wailed. "Why did you let my Dad die in prison? Everyone knows about it now. Everyone knows what he did. I didn't want this.'

Yet surely, that was the whole point. The world knew what he had done and so his power was gone. Those vicious relatives who had accused me of breaking the family could not have been further from the truth. The court case against Grampy was about stopping the rot and starting the healing. It was not about seeing Grampy jailed, although that was the safest place for him and for the rest of us. It was about breaking the chain so future generations would be safe and would know that abuse was always, always, always, wrong.

The fact he died in prison was his own fault and nobody else's. If I kept telling myself that, I hoped I'd one day believe it. And my guilt was quickly replaced by resentment when I learned his funeral was to be paid for by the state. He was entitled to a free send-off, but my mother, his victim, was not. It was yet another fundamental flaw in a system which put victims as the last priority at every opportunity. I of course did not attend the funeral, but some of my relatives went, which left me more disillusioned than dumfounded. I did not mourn Grampy but neither did I celebrate his death. There was no victory for anyone here.

22

WHILST GRIEVING Mum, I'd adopted a little dog, a white and apricot Maltese Cavachon who Shania named Pugsey. I'd been an animal lover ever since my first pet, Hammy, and my heart had never quite healed from losing him. From having my own place, aged 16, I'd always had dogs, and I loved them all. But Pugsey was special. From the first moment I met him at the breeder's home, he ran to my feet and barked importantly, as if to say: 'You'll do for me. I'm coming home with you.'

Pugsey was a delight. In character, the kids pointed out he was very similar to me; strong-willed and outspoken, but hopelessly soft-hearted. He had a firm moral code too. If he was naughty, he'd put himself in his cage with his head hanging and his mouth turned down, as if he was saying: 'Sorry Mum, I've let myself down. I won't do it again.'

Pugsey picked up immediately that I was going through a bad time. He sensed my grief and anxiety and did his best to comfort me. If my mood dipped, he was right there beside me, snuggled on the sofa or nestled on the pillow in bed.

Even whilst I was cooking dinner, he'd follow me around the kitchen like a miniature shadow, quickly realising that I needed him even more than he needed me. On my darkest days, Pugsey never left my side. He knew, even before me, when I was about to cry. I might be sitting on the edge of the bath, with tears stinging behind my eyes, and I would hear his little paws pattering up the stairs to find me. He would look at me with his big, wise eyes and I felt suddenly calmer. It was like magic.

"This dog is more human than any of us," I declared. "He's a gift from another world."

Sometimes, I wondered if Mum had sent him herself to cheer me up. One night, in the summer of 2023, we were all watching a film at home. Pugsey was usually quite happy to squash in alongside me on the sofa. But that night, he was pacing up and down the living room, unable to settle, as though something was worrying him. When I picked him up, I felt his little heart racing through my fingers.

"He's not well," I frowned. "I can just tell."

Brandon suggested we cook him a steak to test his appetite, and when he wolfed it down, I felt a little better. But during the night, he began pacing again. His heart rate felt so fast, I decided to call the vet.

"Bring him in," the vet said, when I described his symptoms.

Usually Pugsey liked to stick his head out of the passenger window in the car so he could see everyone passing and throw out a friendly bark. But when I strapped him in, he just lay on the seat and looked mournfully into my eyes. I had a horrible feeling he was trying to tell me something. At the vets, he had tests and was quickly diagnosed with a heart murmur.

"I'm afraid he's not going to get better," the vet said. "I'm sorry. The kindest thing would be to let him go."

In shock, I ran from the surgery and out into the night air.

"Please, no," I begged, as the tears streamed down my face. "Don't take my Pugsey."

The vet came outside to find me.

"I knew you were crying, because Pugsey started crying too," she told me. "He's very in tune with your emotions."

I couldn't bear the thought that I was upsetting him. Drawing on all my inner strength, I dried my eyes and went back into the consulting room. Moments later, I cradled him on my knee as he slipped away. He was eight years old. In his short life, he had brought us immense and immeasurable joy and happiness.

"Pugsey, I love you," I whispered, as he took his last breath. "And thank you."

I had been through so much loss in my life, yet I felt Pugsey's passing all the more keenly for it. He was a treasured family member, much more than a pet, and I miss him still today. A couple of months later, Maverick, our British shorthaired tabby cat, was knocked down and killed. It was another heart-wrenching loss.

"Bad luck comes in threes," I said sadly. "What's next?"

In November 2023, I did a pregnancy test and found out Christian and I were having a baby. It was a big surprise, but I was nonetheless pleased. I couldn't wait to be a mum again. One morning in early December, at around seven weeks pregnant, I woke with painful stomach cramps. When I saw the blood-stained sheets, my heart stuttered. Once again, I was a small child, shivering in bathwater, tinged pink with blood. Once again, I was a frightened teenager, praying for baby Acacia to survive as I was rushed to hospital.

"Not again," I gasped. "Please, don't let it happen again."

Brandon called an ambulance, but we were told there were long delays of up to nine hours. Eventually, I dragged myself out of bed and drove myself to hospital. By the time I arrived, my leggings were blood-soaked.

"I think I'm having a miscarriage," I told the receptionist tearfully.

After I was examined, a doctor confirmed my fears.

"I'm so sorry," he said.

I was admitted to hospital overnight and allowed home the next day. Alongside the sadness at losing my baby, I was again grieving Acacia and the miscarriage raked up more distressing memories from the past. It hurt me both that I did not know where her remains were buried, and also that I had not, as a frightened teenager, had the courage to ask. Christmas that year was subdued. I was always an over-giver at the festive season, compensating for the lack of extended family and keen to paper over the cracks from my own childhood. But this year, despite my efforts, we could not truly celebrate. The kids had been looking forward to a new addition to the family, and they grieved as I did. The loss of our baby was an irreparable blow for Christian and me and sadly we decided to separate.

Into 2024, I made the decision to apply for my social services and medical records. I had vivid memories from my childhood, but I had many confusing gaps too. Those early years squatted in my soul, one dense block of anxiety, and I could no longer ignore them. I hadn't a single photo of myself as a child; I didn't know what I'd looked like or who I really was. And even with those clearest memories, I had only a child's perspective; I wanted another point of view. Seen from different angles, a painting can mean different things to different people. I was hoping for another angle on my childhood, and I was also hoping for explanations. The notes finally came through at the end of the year but many of the social services records from my early years had, disappointingly, been lost or were unavailable. Those from later years made excruciating reading and I could only allow myself to read one page at a time. One heart-wrenching entry in my medical records from July 2008 read: 'suicidal, unable to eat or drink… difficult upbringing… big family, not willing to help each other…'

The doctor noted that I had: 'good insight' which, I saw now, was as much a curse as a blessing.

Other records stated: 'parents are drug addicts. Dad bullied her.'

And in 2015 – the worst year of my life – the records said: 'Mother murdered last week – had to identify the body yesterday. Understandably in shock, anxiety, and nightmares and distress. Brother is currently in care and coming to live with her from Monday. No family support. (avoids them due to drugs etc.)'

Seeing Mum's murder recorded so matter-of-factly was a punch to the gut. I closed my eyes and saw again those trees waving in the breeze as she lay dying beneath them. I felt the ice-cold finality of her fingers in mine at the morgue. I heard her voice, pushing into my dreams:

'Tar, why did you send my dad to jail? Why did you do it?'

With my head in my hands, I wailed against my pain and loss. How had it all gone so wrong? How could the actions of one man destroy so much? I felt a hot swell of anger towards Grampy, followed by familiar twinges of guilt and shame. Why, in all this horrible mess, could I not just experience one feeling at a time? Why was I flooded with so many clashing and conflicting emotions?

On every page of my notes, there were references to family difficulties, abuse, neglect and addiction. Even on paper, I felt a pinch of shame at my family's inadequacies and failings. As a unit, we were doomed to fail. I saw that clearly now. Over and over, in my medical notes, I had spoken of wanting to die and of no longer being able to cope. My heart splintered into pieces for that poor, lonely young woman who was so racked with responsibility and anxiety that she could not carry on. I wanted to reach onto the page and give her a hug. But it was too late now.

"How am I still here?" I sobbed, as yet another doctor wrote that I was suicidal. "How did I make it this far?"

There were entries too which referred to my nose injury after Dad had punched me as a child: 'Breathing problems. Bullied for nose. Gets panic attacks re nose.'

Like my skin condition, my nose was a physical emblem of all that was wrong within my family and inside my head. Reading my notes stirred up a sadness and anger which I had hoped was long buried. Like the abuse, I had tried to compartmentalise my childhood neglect hoping, in vain, it might simply vaporise of its own accord. Instead, hidden away, it had festered and calcified. Like a malignancy, it was growing and dragging me down. I grieved for that little girl, for the childhood I'd never had, for the happiness and security I'd never known. On Christmas Eve 2024, I broke down. I couldn't stop crying. I ran myself a bath, which was usually calming, but the tears flowed faster still. The ghosts of Christmases past crowded my head and I remembered my pink diary with the lock and key. And how it had been my only friend.

"How have I survived this far?" I sobbed.

I spent most of the day on the phone to a mental health crisis team. Somehow, with the love from my children, I managed to muddle through Christmas Day. In the New Year, I was referred for counselling but was warned there were long delays.

"You might wait a year or more," I was told.

That felt so unfair. If I had been addicted to drugs or alcohol, or my children were going into care, I'd have received help as an emergency. But my reward for working hard and keeping my family together was to sit uncomplainingly at the back of the queue. It was unacceptable. I was being punished for trying to take responsibility; my parents had done that to me all through my childhood, and now the system was penalising me as well. I didn't want pity or charity. Yet I did need support. But from a young age, I'd learned to cope on my own, and I knew I could do it again.

At first, I was unable to leave the house. I suffered with panic attacks and anxiety. When I finally felt strong enough to drive, months later, Brandon sat in the passenger seat with his hand on my shoulder. It was such a small gesture, but it meant the world to me.

'This will pass,' I told myself. 'Tomorrow will come.'

23

IN FEBRUARY 2025, tougher and stronger, I was accepted onto an Open University degree course to study psychology and counselling.

For a girl with 12% school attendance, who left without a single GCSE, it felt like quite an achievement. For so long, it had been my dream to help others. Even as a little girl, studying Mum's face instead of watching TV, my inner psychologist was taking root. My request to meet the Gassman killers came from a desire to understand what motivated them to take Mum's life. Even when Grampy was jailed, I focussed on why and how and not on the true horror of what he did.

I'd always been fascinated by how others behaved, and so this was the perfect choice for me. It was not easy, studying at degree level when I didn't even have GCSEs. I relied heavily on Brandon and Shania as sounding boards for my essays and my presentations. Sometimes, in class, I found myself furtively looking up words I didn't understand! But as time went on, it became easier and more rewarding.

In October 2025, I began training as a volunteer with Support After Murder and Manslaughter (SAMM). I want to help other families who have suffered like mine. I also volunteer with Swansea Women's Aid, sending Christmas boxes to families in hostels. That was me once and I won't ever forget how lonely it was.

As Spring 2026 arrives, I'm still on the endless waiting list for my own counselling. There are some childhood memories I might never retrieve. I don't understand why my blood turns to ice when I think of the toy bus and the yellow teapot under Grampy's stairs. But life is not about full circles. It's about getting through the day. Not everything can be neatly rounded off and parcelled away.

My view of relationships has, for many years, been discoloured by abuse but earlier this year, I fell in love. My partner, Liam has held my hand through writing this book and cathartically reliving the pain. The sharp edges of grief and trauma have softened now, and I can wake each morning without that piercing, heart-rending agony. I'm learning to live with my losses. I know, without argument, that I did the right thing in helping to jail my grandfather and to break the chain which was poisoning the future generations of our family.

I understand too it was the correct decision to move to Swansea and separate myself from many of my family members. I think the decision saved my life, and certainly, it saved my children. My self-image and self-confidence have improved. I will always have hang-ups, physically and mentally. I have had laser treatment on my skin to hide the scars from my teenage acne. I've had two surgeries on my nose, to improve the shape and also my breathing. Though these procedures were successful, I still look in the mirror and find fault. But I can accept the problem is mostly in my mind.

My greatest pride is my family. We have two little dogs, Arlo, a Cavapoochon, who is completely daft but lovely, and also Enzo, a Chorkie, who is more of a show off. He performs tricks and unfortunately also eats our shoes, our underwear, our cushions and carpets!

Cameron, now 22, has his own place nearby with his girlfriend and we see him regularly. I am so proud of the wonderful young man he has become, he's one of the best. Brandon and Shania still live at home. Brandon is training as a plumber and electrician. He has my stubbornness, but he is gentle and affectionate too. Shania is at college studying criminology, and she is strong and resilient. If I was ever sick in bed, Brandon would be bringing me lemon and honey whilst Shania would be telling me to get up and think positive! They balance each other so well. The irony is, I never stay in bed even when I'm ill, because I worry that I'm failing them. Illogically, I link getting the flu with being a bad parent. There are some irrationalities I just can't shake. I'm a self-diagnosed helicopter parent too. I am guilty, if there is such a thing, of loving Brandon and Shania too much and being too proud of them!

I still speak to Mum most days. I have a picture of my parents in my living room and, as I am dusting and polishing, I like to blow them both a kiss. The time for judgement has long passed.

"I know you struggled, I know you did your best, and I love you," I say.

Every time I hear a Carpenters song, I smile. Sometimes, I can hear Mum's voice in mine. I might tell a joke, and I think of her. I hope she is proud of me at last for putting a paedophile behind bars. Like a mother, I did not do what she wanted but what was best for her. Despite her many struggles, if I had a second chance at life, I would choose my mother again. Her suffering gave me strength, and her trauma lit a fire within me. Thanks to her, I understand that everything passes, and that tomorrow will come.

Time marches on and even the most painful moments are usurped by those which follow. Nothing lasts for ever and if we all carried hate and bitterness around, where would it end? The world needs love. Start by loving those closest to you, and radiate outwards. I will not live in the dark. I am a warrior and a survivor, and my pain is my path to brightness.

Acknowledgements

THANKS TO all who carried me and believed in me whilst going back through my timelines and facing my demons.

Ann Cusack for believing and seeing something in me to make this platform possible.

Pugsey-dog for showing me the purest love in my life and licking away the tears.

My kids Brandon, Shania and brother Cameron – for holding my heart and giving me the strength to forever fight and make a change. Your pure love showed me the true mother and sister I am and forever will be. You all give me the reasons to get up every day and fight.

My partner Liam Widlake – for holding and carrying me in the dark times.

To my siblings – without you, and my upbringing, I would never have found my inner fight xxx

Other bestselling Mirror Books

Abandoned

Monica Allan

With Ann Cusack

Monica was just five years old when her mother tried to kill her by forcing her head under running bathroom taps. She had already tried to strangle her as a baby

Escaping into foster care, Monica would go on to experience horrific physical and sexual abuse at the hands of those she hoped would protect her. She tried to find a new life and raise a loving family of her own. But living with the devastating secrets that had been buried for so long proved too painful.

Enough was enough. To live again, she knew she had to confront the demons of her past.

MIRROR BOOKS

The Asylum

Carol Minto

With Ann Cusack

For 46 years, Carol Minto has quietly gone about her life, carrying with her the most extraordinary and heartbreaking secrets.

Born into poverty and with mostly absent parents, Carol helped to raise her nine siblings. But when she was just 11 years old, her older brother began to sexually abuse her. After four years, Carol managed to escape – and ran away from home.

In *The Asylum* Carol tells the full story of how she overcame unimaginable suffering, to find the happiness and solace she has today as a mother and grandmother.

MIRROR BOOKS